THE COMMONWEALTH AND INTERNATIONAL LIBRARY
Joint Chairmen of the Honorary Editorial Advisory Board
SIR ROBERT ROBINSON, O.M., F.R.S., LONDON
DEAN ATHELSTAN SPILHAUS, MINNESOTA

PSYCHOLOGY DIVISION

A Students' Guide to Piaget

A Students' Guide
to Piaget

BY

D. G. BOYLE, B.Sc., Ph. D.

Lecturer in Psychology in the University of Leeds

PERGAMON PRESS

Oxford · New York · Toronto · Sydney · Braunschweig

Pergamon Press Ltd., Headington Hill Hall, Oxford

Pergamon Press Inc., Maxwell House, Fairview Park, Elmsford,
New York 10523

Pergamon of Canada Ltd., 207 Queen's Quay West, Toronto 1

Pergamon Press (Aust.) Pty. Ltd., 19a Boundary Street, Rushcutters Bay,
N.S.W. 2011, Australia

Vieweg & Sohn GmbH, Burgplatz 1, Braunschweig

First edition 1969

Reprinted 1970

Library of Congress Catalog Card No. 77–94056

Printed in Great Britain by A. Wheaton & Co., Exeter

08 006406 x (flexicover)
08 006407 8 (hard cover)

Contents

III EPISTEMOLOGY AND PSYCHOLOGY

IV PERSPECTIVE

Preface

NATHAN ISAACS, in *Some Aspects of Piaget's Work*, remarks that we need an "Intelligent Students' Guide to Piaget". The fact that the adjective "intelligent" does not appear in my title does not, of course, mean that this book is intended for unintelligent students. It was simply that my book was well advanced before I came across Mr. Isaacs's suggestion. However, it encourages me to learn that a distinguished Piagetian scholar feels, as I do, that a book making Piaget's ideas more accessible to non-specialists may be welcome.

I have not attempted to give a systematic exposition of the whole of Piaget's work. That is not necessary, as Flavell has recently done this in *The Developmental Psychology of Jean Piaget;* indeed, had Flavell not written his book I should have been greatly handicapped in writing mine (readers familiar with this field will also discover the influence of Baldwin's *Theories of Child Development*). However, Flavell explicitly assumes a knowledge of epistemology on the part of his readers, whereas I believe that it is precisely a lack of acquaintance with epistemological ideas that prevents students from appreciating Piaget's work. For this reason I have emphasized Piaget's epistemological work. Inasmuch as my primary aim has been to give a brief exposition for psychology students, I have not attempted to discuss all aspects of Piaget's multifarious epistemological interests. Whilst Piagetian specialists may feel that the picture has been over-simplified, it has seemed to me right, in the interests of clarity of exposition, to restrict the treatment to the minimum necessary to provide a clear framework for psychologists. For this reason I have made no attempt to relate Piaget's epistemology to the views of other European and British philosophers.

In writing this book I have been greatly aided by discussions with my colleagues in the Psychology Department of Leeds University, and I must express particular gratitude to Professor Meredith, who first encouraged me to write this book. With respect to Chapter 9, I was much assisted by the kindness of Dr. K. Lovell, who sent me a copy of a chapter that he is contributing to a forthcoming book. For preparing the typescript for publication my thanks go to Mrs. Margaret Greaves, and the Misses Noreen Giddens and Margaret Morrison.

I owe an incalculable debt to my wife, who not only gave me great encouragement to continue writing when my enthusiasm was flagging, but also read every chapter in manuscript and made many valuable suggestions for improving the clarity of exposition.

I am indebted to the following authors and publishers for permission to quote from their works:

To Professor Jean Piaget and the Manchester University Press for a quotation from *Logic and Psychology*. (Chapter 2.)

To J. M. Dent & Sons Limited, publishers of Jerome K. Jerome, for a passage from *Idle Thoughts of an Idle Fellow*. (Chapter 4.)

To Professor Morris Kline and the Oxford University Press (New York) for a quotation from *Mathematics in Western Culture*. (Chapter 4.)

To Dr. R. S. Peters and George Allen & Unwin Limited, for a quotation from *Ethics and Education*. (Chapter 10.)

D.G.B.

List of Symbols Used

√   square root
>   greater than
+   plus
—   minus
=   equals
⊃   logical implication (e.g. $p \supset q$; p implies q)
∨   disjunction (e.g. $p \vee q$; either p or q)
.   conjunction (e.g. $p.q$; both p and q)
–   negation (e.g. $\bar{p}$; not–p)
/   incompatibilty [e.g. $(p \supset q)/(p.\bar{q})$; "$p$ implies q" is
    incompatible with the truth of p and the falsity of q]

I

GENETIC EPISTEMOLOGY

CHAPTER 1

The Problems to be Solved

THIS book is intended as a guide for students to the work of one of the most influential thinkers in contemporary psychology, and so it is as well that we should start with the major problem that confronts students when they first encounter Piaget's work. The students find little difficulty in following *what* he has done, but they seldom understand *why* he has done it. If one does not understand the *why* of Piaget's work, one cannot grasp the relationship between the facts that Piaget gives and the theory that he derives from them. This book is intended to answer the question "Why?" Piaget is attempting to answer some very important questions in the branch of philosophy called "epistemology". In this chapter we shall try to show what he means by this.

First we must explain what epistemology is about. Put very briefly, epistemology is a study of the limits of knowledge. It addresses itself to such questions as "In what sense can we say that we know anything?" A study of what we know about the intellect, for example, is the province of psychology: consideration of how we are to describe that knowledge is epistemology.

Until the eighteenth century, psychology and philosophy were not clearly distinguished, and many of the questions to which major philosophers of the past attempted to give answers were questions that we should today regard as problems for psychologists. One of these questions was whether the mind at birth is a blank sheet, or *tabula rasa*, on which experience—and experience alone—writes, or whether the mind has an existence, and laws, of its own. These two viewpoints are known to psychologists as the "empiricist" and "nativist" views respectively. Questions of this sort are not resolvable by empirical evidence, but we can conceive of ways in which empirical evidence would be relevant: for instance, if the overwhelming majority of experimental facts could be more satisfactorily explained in terms of one rather than the other viewpoint, then the one yielding the more satisfactory explanations would be more acceptable to scientists. Since this is not so, the point of view that we adopt depends largely on our philosophical outlook which, whether we are aware of it or not, is influenced by the arguments of the great philosophers of the past.

There are other questions to which empirical evidence seems even less relevant. One of the most important of these questions concerns the nature of mathematical entities such as infinite numbers, or the square root of -1. At one time in the history of mathematics these ideas were not part of the science, so how did they come into being? Did Cantor "discover" infinite numbers in a vision, as he claimed? Was $\sqrt{-1}$ "discovered" or was it "invented"? If it was invented, what does "invention" mean in this context? These questions are the province of *mathematical epistemology*, and they have exercised the greatest minds of Western civilization since the days of Plato and Aristotle. The reason for this great interest is that mathematical knowledge (and, in particular, geometry) comprises a body of deductions from self-evident axioms and is therefore indisputably true: at the same time these deductions are more than mere tautologies, and mathematical study really does tell us things that we did not know before. For example, starting from the axioms of Euclidean geometry (which are self-evidently true), we can deduce that the angle inscribed in a semicircle is a right angle (which is undeniably true but by no means self-evident).

Geometry thus poses a paradox. The theorems constitute new knowledge, yet this knowledge consists of deductions from self-evident truths such as "the whole is greater than any of its parts" and "any two points may be connected by a straight line". In what sense, then, is mathematical knowledge "new"? The major part of Piaget's work may be interpreted as an attempt to answer questions of this sort. Piaget takes the view that a fruitful approach to understanding the problems of knowledge is by **way** of a study of the genesis of intellectual structures in man, hence *genetic* epistemology. He originally intended to spend approximately 5 years studying the development of intelligence in the child, but in fact devoted 40 years to the problem.

In the rest of this chapter we shall attempt to state the problems of mathematical epistemology as philosophers have seen them, and summarize the various types of answer that they have given.* Then we shall indicate the nature of Piaget's answer, developing this theme in succeeding chapters before attempting an evaluation of Piaget's contribution to psychology.

Let us start by considering a triangle. There is one sure thing that we can say about a triangle, namely that the sum of its internal angles equals two right angles. If one tries to demonstrate this by drawing a triangle and deriving the proof, one finds that the triangle that has been drawn has other properties: for example it may be equilateral or isosceles or right-angle. Even if one is careful to draw a scalene triangle, the particular triangle that one has drawn will have specific properties that other triangles have not. Of what triangle are we talking when we say that the sum of the angles equals two right angles? Clearly we are talking about triangles in general, but we have performed our reasoning about one particular triangle. René Descartes (1596–1650) argued that our minds work in such a way that they form general propositions from a knowledge of particular cases. Whilst this suggestion is highly plausible, it is open to the objection that our propositions about triangles seem indisputably true, whereas if they were formed from reasoning about individual triangles, it is conceivable that one day we should come across a triangle whose angles did not sum to two right angles.

Two solutions to the difficulty were offered by the British Empiricists John Locke (1632–1704) and George Berkeley (1685–1753). Locke suggested that our geometrical reasoning is

---

* The rest of this chapter is based on Part One of *Mathematical Epistemology and Psychology* by E. W. Beth and J. Piaget (see the bibliography for details.)

performed upon a *general triangle*, which is neither right-angled, nor equilateral, nor isosceles, nor scalene. Formulations of this sort have seldom proved as helpful in clarifying thinking as their formulators intended, and Berkeley proposed an alternative solution. Berkeley's solution was to propose that, when we demonstrate a theorem about a particular triangle we make no mention in the proof of the specific properties of that particular triangle. Hence we are entitled to generalize from particulars to the general case.

Two questions are involved in this discussion, the first being "Why do we need to perform our reasoning upon a particular example, rather than deduce theorems directly from axioms without an intermediate step?" Descartes's proposal about how the mind works is an answer to this question. It does not satisfactorily answer the second question, which is "How can an argument about a particular triangle yield a general conclusion?" Locke's suggestion that we reason about a "general triangle" is an answer to this second question, as is Berkeley's proposal that, in the proof of a theorem, we mention only the features of general relevance.

The third member of the trio of British Empiricists, David Hume (1711–76), commented on the psychological aspect of the problem. He observed that when we reason about a particular triangle we are led to think about other triangles that differ from the one in front of us. If, say, we have formulated a general conclusion about a triangle that is equilateral, the thought of an isosceles triangle may cause us to realize that our conclusion is not as general as we first thought, and we may revise our conclusion. Then thinking of a scalene triangle may make us realize that our revised conclusion applies only to equilateral and isosceles triangles. In this way we progressively refine our conclusion until we have arrived at a satisfactory formulation. Hume is describing a dialectical argument, and his suggestion is a reply to the first question rather than the second because it is not clear that we could ever be *certain* of our conclusions, however long we continued our dialectical reasoning, for it is always conceivable that someone could produce an example that we had not considered. The characteristic certainty of mathematics is still not accounted for.

Hume's German contemporary Immanuel Kant (1724–1804) attempted a synthesis of previous views by arguing that mathematical demonstrations bring out what is involved in our conception of a triangle. This conception does not depend upon experience but is the result of intuition; mathematical definitions are *constructions* that give form and substance to the concepts framed by the mind. Intuition, in addition to ensuring that the concepts that the mind frames are significant rather than trivial, guides the process of mathematical reasoning, thus ensuring that demonstrations are valid rather than spurious.

The question of intuition requires careful examination. Euclid's geometry is founded upon ten axioms, all of which appear self-evident. Yet two of these axioms worried even Euclid himself. The first of these was the one that states that a line can be extended *ad infinitum* in either direction. The other was the axiom that states that two lines that are parallel will not meet however far they extended; this axiom in particular caused Euclid and later geometers concern. A number of thinkers attempted to derive this axiom from simpler axioms, or else tried to construct geometries with another axiom about parallel lines substituted for Euclid's. One person who succeeded in constructing a valid geometry with a parallel lines axiom different from Euclid's was Karl Friedrich Gauss (1777–1855). Morris Kline (1953) tells us that it was Kant's influence that made Gauss withhold his discoveries from the world. Kant had believed that Euclidean geometry described the way in which the mind apprehends space. Consequently, to postulate a non-Euclidean geometry was, seemingly, to fly in the face of reason. In fact, it is to deny the importance of intuition in guiding the selection of axioms. The establishment of non-Euclidean geometries by Lobachevsky (1826), Bolyai (1823), and Riemann (1855) undermined Kant's views on the role of intuition in mathematical reasoning.

It remains true that most people feel happier about these new geometries when their theorems are related to the subjective experience of space. It can, in fact, be shown that, whereas Euclid's geometry provides the best description of a plane surface, the geometry of Lobachevsky and Bolyai more satisfactorily describes a cylindrical surface, and Riemann's geometry a sphere (Kline, 1953, ch. 26). In view of the need that most people feel for spatial demonstration of geometrical theorems, it is not surprising that there is a long tradition of attempts to explain logical and mathematical reasoning in psychological terms.

One of the best known representatives of this tradition is John Stuart Mill (1806—73). Mill's solution of the problem as to why logical and mathematical truths appear both necessarily true and informative was to propose that they are not "truths" at all, but inductive generalizations based on a very large number of instances. Thus we never find a triangle whose angles do not sum to 180 degrees (or approximately 180 degrees, the differences being due to contingencies of constructing an actual triangle), and so our mind is incapable of conceiving that things could be otherwise. This view accounts for the feeling of necessity in terms of the limitations of our minds, which is a psychological criterion. Mill took a similar view with regard to the laws of logic, for instance "no proposition can be simultaneously true and untrue"; he held that the apparent necessity of this law was due to the inability of the mind to conceive the simultaneous truth and falsity of a proposition.

Mill, in fact, believed logic and psychology to be inseparable, and held that we can only understand the validity of logical rules on the basis of a study of the psychology of belief. However, Mill's psychology was speculative rather than empirical, and the psychology of belief has not confirmed Mill's picture of man's rationality.

Mill's arguments have also been attacked on logical grounds. Put very briefly, the current view of the necessary nature of logical and mathematical truths is that they are true simply because we do not allow them to be otherwise. For instance, the reason why the internal angles of all triangles sum to two right angles is that part of the procedure for identifying a triangle is the procedure for determining that the sum of the interior angles is 180 degrees. If we discovered a triangle whose angles summed to 179 degrees, we should assume that we had measured incorrectly or that the figure did not have the properties of a Euclidean triangle. To put it another way, the truth of our theorems is guaranteed by the rule that we follow in employing our axioms.*

Opposed to the tradition of psychological explanation of logicomathematical laws has been the tradition of explanation in terms of logic, which is currently believed to be correct. This tradition goes back to Aristotle who held that a demonstrative science must be based on *primitive notions* (such as point, line, and so on) and *primitive truths* (that is to say, axioms). Aristotle believed that we are directly acquainted with these primitive notions by intuition. We never encounter, in the world that we perceive, points with no area, infinitely long lines, and so on; but our intuition enables us to discern, in our percepts, the operation of principles based upon the primitive notions. We develop the consequences of these principles by the faculty of reason.

To make Aristotle's position clear, we must mention the ways in which he differed from Plato, who preceded him, and from Descartes and Kant, who followed him. Plato believed that the entities of mathematics belong to a realm of reality distinct from the perceptible world: Aristotle argued that we study perceptible objects, but disregard inessential properties (such as weight and colour), thus deriving the entities of mathematics by abstraction. Aristotle held that demonstrative sciences involve both intuition and reason: Descartes and Kant attempted to reduce mathematical knowledge solely to intuition.

One of the most important thinkers in this tradition was Gottfried Wilhelm von Leibniz (1646–1716), who attempted to found mathematics on logic. Leibniz argued that, whilst we cannot eliminate all assumptions about axioms, we can attempt to reduce

* Ayer (1946), pp. 73–75, and Britton (1953), ch. 4.

axioms to the simplest possible terms, for example tautologies. We may illustrate Leibniz's argument (and the limitations of this approach) by means of his attempt to demonstrate that $2 + 2 = 4$, given that $4 = 3 + 1$. The only axiom that Leibniz allows is that "by putting equals in the place of equals, equality remains". We proceed by means of this axiom and three definitions as follows:

Definitions		
	$2 = 1 + 1$	(definition 1)
	$3 = 2 + 1$	(definition 2)
	$4 = 3 + 1$	(definition 3)

Demonstration		
	$2 + 2 = 2 + 1 + 1$	(from definition 1)
	$2 + 1 + 1 = 3 + 1$	(from definition 2)
	$3 + 1 = 4$	(from definition 3)

Conclusion		
	$2 + 2 = 4$	(from the axiom)

Unfortunately this reasoning is not complete. The demonstration assumes that $2 + (1 + 1)$ in the first line of the demonstration is the same as $(2 + 1) + 1$ in the second line. We are not entitled to assume this, so to make the demonstration complete we must state a second axiom, namely that $2 + (1 + 1) = (2 + 1) + 1$, or, in more general terms, $(a + b) + c = a + (b + c)$. This second axiom, which defines the property known as "associativity" (that is to say, that the sum of a set of numbers is independent of the order in which they are added) is not a tautology.

Although Leibniz's attempts to found mathematics on logic failed, he saw clearly the conditions that must be met if such a programme is to succeed. One of these conditions is the construction of a formalized language in terms of which pure logic can be rigorously expressed. We cannot here follow the development of this programme but must be limited to the observation that, in our own day, the work of Bertrand Russell has caused some philosophers to doubt that mathematics can be reduced to pure logic, at least as logic has been traditionally conceived.

(To anticipate a point to be developed later, one of the most significant aspects of Piaget's work is his attempt to synthesize the contributions of the logical and psychological traditions in mathematical epistemology.)

In many ways the most puzzling aspect of the nature of logico-mathematical axioms is this: given the axioms, we may derive theorems from them with a high degree of rigour, yet we can find no way of rigorously demonstrating that the axioms are justified. It appears, therefore, that even the most nearly perfect form of human reasoning is incomplete. This realization was first made explicit by Blaise Pascal (1623–62). Another version of this puzzle is found with respect to progress in mathematics. Progress occurs when mathematicians solve problems that were previously not solved, and problem solving is of very great interest to psychologists. Two mathematicians whose introspections on their methods of solving problems are reproduced in nearly every introductory textbook in psychology were Henri Poincaré and Jacques Hadamard. (Ghiselin (ed.), 1952.) As a result of their introspections, we accept that unconscious mental activity plays a crucial role in problem solving. The unconscious work must be preceded by conscious preparation, and is ended by a sudden illumination, which often comes when one is engaged in some entirely different activity. Then follows further conscious work, by which one tests the inspiration yielded by the unconscious. We may therefore describe the process of problem solving as comprising four stages, namely;

1. Preparation.   3. Inspiration.
2. Incubation.   4. Verification.

The paradox is this. The preparation consists of a study of all aspects of the problem in the light of what we know already. The verification consists of testing, in the most rigorous manner possible, the insight yielded by the unconscious. Yet the unconscious yields new knowledge, apparently in disregard of the rigorous methods characteristic of mathematical demonstration. A number of resolutions have been proposed of this paradox, including the suggestion that the solution only *seems* to arise suddenly; that in fact the unconscious reviews every possible solution that has been looked at, however briefly, in the period of conscious preparation, and erases from consciousness all except the correct one. However, none of these proposals can escape the fact that the unconscious plays an active part in problem solving.

Inasmuch as the unconscious can only play an effective role if the periods of conscious work are also successful, mathematicians have made a number of attempts to formulate a mathematical *heuristic*, that is a set of rules to be followed to ensure success in problem solving. Now the heuristic procedures to be followed in the period of preparation are different from the heuristic procedures of the period of verification. The first set guides the mathematician in his general approach (for instance he should read as widely as possible about the problem and should make as many attempts to solve it, in different ways, as he can, before laying the problem aside), whereas the second set of rules has the power to demonstrate the truths of the solution. When we solve a problem in arithmetic we adopt a procedure that combines both these aspects, because if we make a number of different attempts at solution, we eventually arrive at an answer, and so long as we have followed the rules of arithmetic, our answer will be correct. However, solving an arithmetical problem is not the same sort of activity as solving a problem that contributes to the advance of mathematics. With this sort of problem it appears to be impossible to find one set of heuristic procedures that both guides invention and has demonstrative power.

Once more, then, we find that it is possible to demonstrate with great rigour the truth of a solution once we have it (just as we may derive a theorem rigorously from axioms), but we cannot rigorously ensure that we arrive at a solution (any more than we can demonstrate the truth of our axioms). We now see more clearly the point of the question raised earlier in this chapter, namely whether mathematical entities are invented or discovered. Plato believed that mathematics deals with objects that are beyond the visible world. Later mathematicians who have shared

Plato's view have believed that mathematical progress consists of *discovering* solutions, whilst others have held that mathematicians *invent* them. Piaget, as we shall show, believes that there is a third possibility, namely that we *construct* solutions which, if they are valid, conform to the laws of the human intellect, and hence to the laws of nature, inasmuch as human beings are part of nature.

Consideration of the nature of mathematics is the province of philosophy, but Piaget believes that psychology may contribute greatly to philosophy in this respect. However, the problem of more direct and obvious concern to psychologists as such concerns the nature of the mathematician's *activity*, such as the conscious and unconscious work that we have already mentioned. It will be instructive to pursue this topic a little further.

Everyone is familiar with Zeno's paradox about Achilles and the tortoise. It may be stated as follows. Achilles gives the tortoise a start of 100 yards, then starts running ten times as fast as the tortoise. When Achilles has covered 100 yards, the tortoise has travelled 10 yards. By the time Achilles has travelled 10 yards, the tortoise has covered 1 yard, so after Achilles has run 110 yards, the tortoise is 1 yard ahead. Achilles can never, in fact catch the tortoise, because by the time he has run this yard, the tortoise has travelled a further one-tenth of a yard, and so on.

Now clearly this is absurd. We know that Achilles *will* catch up with the tortoise, so what is wrong with our reasoning? The answer is that it is illegitimate to think of time and space as divisible into units, which was the philosophy underlying the arithmetic of Eudoxus whose views Zeno was challenging. This approach is known at *atomism*, and it may be thought that mathematicians would have dropped this approach in view of the paradoxes to which it gave rise. In fact, the approach was revived in the sixteenth century and made possible the development of calculus. Thus, ideas are not necessarily abandoned, even when they lead to paradoxes: mathematicians will still employ them if they lead to valuable techniques.

This fact raises two very interesting questions. First, "Why do mathematicians continue to employ approaches that have been shown to lead to paradoxes?" The second question is "Since the basis of their reasoning is unsatisfactory, how do they ensure that their results are correct?"

These questions are special forms of the more general question, which we have already touched upon, namely "Why are there different heuristic procedures for guiding invention and demonstrating the truth of a solution?" As a preliminary answer we may say that, if a technique proves valuable, mathematicians will not wait to use it until its validity has been rigorously demonstrated; in the case of calculus, for example, it was not until 1821 that a satisfactory account was given of its basis (Kline, 1953, ch. 15). To anticipate once more, we shall see that Piaget's answer will be that demonstration must be of a different nature from mathematical construction, because demonstration makes use of the intellectual structures whose establishment is an essential part of construction. Piaget sees the growth of the intellect in the individual as of essentially the same nature as the progress of understanding over the centuries.

One feature of Piaget's work is especially relevant here. Between the ages of 4 and 7 years, children characteristically act as if they understand physical nature even though they cannot explain how they understand. For example, a 5-year-old will know that it is absurd to suppose that one can balance on a bicycle without turning the pedals but will not be able to explain why (nor, for that matter, will most adults). The child behaves as if he has an intuitive grasp of physical realities. This feature of development is strikingly similar to the progress of mathematics in such matters as the development of calculus, and brings us once more to consider the role of intuition in mathematics.

In their efforts to solve problems, contemporary mathematicians frequently make use of spatial intuition: they construct "pictures" or visual models of the problem in terms of which they can understand the solution. This appeal to spatial intuition is a powerful heuristic device. However, when they demonstrate the solution, that is to say, give a *formal* account of it to other mathematicians, they eschew intuition. This was not always so, and in Euclid's *Elements* the demonstrations contain serious *lacunae*. It is generally supposed that the ancient geometers tacitly appealed to spatial intuition to fill in the gaps in their arguments, but despite this they achieved the correct answers. Does this mean that spatial intuition is a reliable source of information? If it is, then are contemporary mathematicians denying themselves access to indispensable information in eschewing the appeal to spatial intuition in their demonstrations, or are they appealing to spatial intuition without being aware of it?

Kant believed that mathematicians appealed unconsciously to spatial intuition, but it is generally accepted today that spatial intuition is not employed in demonstrations. The interesting fact remains that, in the past, spatial intuition *has* played a major role, and so we are obliged to try to explain how an appeal to intuition has given rise to correct theorems. One answer was given by Hermann von Helmholtz (1821–94), who suggested that the fundamental elements of spatial intuition are innate, and permit the spontaneous organization of spatial experiences (students will be familiar with the later development of this point of view in the work of the Gestalt school—see Boring (1950, ch. 23). These innate elements should be compatible with many structures of space, but they are supplemented by empirical elements, that is to say elements derived from experience, which ensure that our organization of space conforms to reality. Poincaré, whom we have already mentioned, remarked that the particular spatial structure that we adopt is partly a matter of convenience.

The difficulty with such conceptions is that our naïve intuition (which probably contains both innate and empirical elements) yields concepts such as "point", "line", and so on, whereas axioms make use of rather different concepts, for instance "point with no magnitude", "line with no breadth". These formal concepts must have been derived from naïve intuition by a process of abstraction or idealization. Consequently, our axioms must be based on primitive notions that are inaccessible to naïve intuition. A number of mathematicians have attempted to resolve this difficulty by constructing sets of axioms on primitive notions with as primitive a nature as possible (for instance, the relation of part to whole) in addition to axioms expressing empirical elements. However, their attempts characteristically seem artificial, and it appears that sets of axioms that are satisfactory from the theoretical point of view are not the most useful for solving practical problems: for this purpose the concepts of naïve intuition are more appropriate.

It would divert us from our main purpose to follow these attempts to construct sets of axioms that do not rely on intuition, but there is a phenomenon in connection with intuition that is of great interest to a psychologist. We have seen that many thinkers, from Aristotle to Kant, felt great concern for the conformity of geometrical concepts with intuitive self-evidence, and that this caused many nineteenth-century geometers to dismiss non-Euclidean geometries as scientifically unacceptable. Today their scientific character is universally accepted. What has happened to make people change their views?

One answer, given by Bernays (Beth and Piaget, 1966, ch. 6), is that self-evidence is not fixed and invariable, but changes with time. The same point is made by Stephen Toulmin, who argues that what scientists regard as a phenomenon (i.e. something to be explained) depends upon their views of the natural order of the universe. These ideas of what is the natural order of things have changed radically in the course of time. For instance, it would seem obvious to us that we could explain the process of ripening by comparing it to a slow form of cooking: Aristotle, on the other hand, would have explained cooking as a speeded-up form of ripening (Toulmin, 1961, chs. 3 and 4). Beth distinguishes the slow incorporation of elements into self-evidence (a reversible process), which he calls "inductive integration", from the sudden and irreversible "noetic integration", which is rare in adults and follows a particularly striking experience. (Presumably when a genius has a noetic integration, he then explains his insight to other thinkers for whom, if he is successful, it becomes an inductive integration.) Piaget, as we shall see in

Chapter 6 of this book, agrees with Beth that this phenomenon is very important for both genetic epistemology and the history of ideas, and has much to say on this topic.

Having outlined, and probably over-simplified, some of the problems of mathematical epistemology, we shall end this chapter with a brief indication of how Piaget proposes to solve these problems in terms of genetic psychology.

Piaget bases his account on his observations of the development of intellectual structures in the human being. The first 2 years are devoted to sensorimotor activity, which is not (except in the first few weeks of life) random, but is organized. The forms that the organization of behaviour takes probably reflect neural organization in the brain. At a later stage in development (from about 7 years), the child is able to deal with his environment without overt action: this is because he has been able to "internalize" his actions in the form of intellectual *operations*. Until he is about 11 years old, however, he still needs to refer to actual objects in order to solve problems, so we may describe his thinking as operational but *concrete*. From 11 years the requirement of concrete support for his thinking diminishes, and he is able to represent problems to himself in terms of their symbolic forms. We may therefore say that he has attained the phase of *formal* operations.

For Piaget, every thought must at some stage in the individual's past history have been an action, although its ancestry will not be obvious because the action will have been transformed in becoming an operation. Forming operations from actions takes place by means of "reflective abstraction", by which Piaget means that the abstracted features are put in a wider context than before, and perform a different function in the intellect.

Just as the child forms operations from actions, the adolescent uses operations as the basis for creating higher order operations, again by "reflective abstraction". The highest achievements of mathematics may be regarded as highly abstract operations attained by a few especially gifted thinkers. Although they are attained by only a few, the process by which they are reached is the reflective abstraction whereby actions are transformed into operations. For Piaget, the mistake made by previous thinkers was to seek the origin of logicomathematical entities either in human nature or in the physical world. Neither is the case, Piaget argues. The origin of these entities is in *the actions that the child performs on objects*. Reflective abstraction starts with abstraction of features of *these actions*, not features of the objects. Therefore neither an examination of the human intellect, nor a study of physical world, can provide an answer to the problems of epistemology: we must study *the intellect in its relationships with the world*. Inasmuch as this relationship is highly complex in the adult (and in mathematicians so abstract that the connection with the physical world is so recondite as to be frequently undetectable), we must study the genesis of this relationship in babies from the moment of birth.

There are two aspects to this approach to the problem. In the first place, one needs to examine the development of intellectual structures: this examination took Piaget 40 years, and the results of his study are summarized in Chapters 2–5 of this book. Secondly, one must show that this genetic study solves the problems of epistemology more convincingly than any other approach: Piaget's solution is summarized in Chapter 6. Clearly it is possible to accept the results of Piaget's developmental research whilst rejecting his epistemological solution; but it is also possible to criticize aspects of the research whilst accepting the general argument. In the present book the exposition and discussion are separated in the interests of clarity of presentation, the discussion occupying Chapters 8–10.

We turn now to an exposition of Piaget's developmental studies.

II

PIAGET'S DEVELOPMENTAL PSYCHOLOGY

CHAPTER 2

The Basic Concepts of Piaget's Psychology

WHEN one realizes that there are many theories of human development, he naturally wonders why. One kind of answer is to be found by analogy with an atlas. An atlas contains three main kinds of map: one shows administrative boundaries; another shows topographical features; a third indicates agricultural and industrial regions. As a rule, all three show certain features, like rivers and towns. In somewhat the same way, a theory of development may indicate "boundaries" of developmental stages (babyhood, the pre-school years, middle childhood, pre-adolescence, puberty, adolescence, maturity) or it may indicate "topographical features" of development (such as weaning, toilet-training, learning to walk and talk). The analogy with maps breaks down a little here, but there are two sorts of topographical features of development: we may look at development primarily from the point of view of motives and their directive influence on emotional growth; or we may look at the growth of the individual's intellect from the point of view of its developing relationships with the world of objects and people around the individual. The first way is Freud's, the second is Piaget's. Admittedly this distinction is over-simple, but it does illustrate the difference of approach.

If one is going to describe the development of the intellect, then two requirements must be satisfied. The first is that all essential features of development must be taken into account (just as different sorts of maps show essential features like rivers and towns). It is here that we find the greatest apparent differences between a Freudian and a Piagetian approach. The Freudian approach is concerned with the vicissitudes of motives: the baby seeks to satisfy its instinctual motives in a different way from the child, and the child in a different way from the adolescent and the adult, but they are basically the same motives—only the objects that satisfy the motives are different. Piaget is concerned with the structure and working of the adult mind, and *how it got that way*. To use another analogy, Freud puts a climber at the foot of the mountain and tells us how he will get to the top: Piaget's climber is at the summit, and Piaget tells us how he got there. Of course, both Freud and Piaget realize that not everyone gets to the top: many will get stuck (fixated) on the way, and some will fall off (and go mad).

The second requirement is a vocabulary for describing the structure of the adult intellect that will also be useful in describing the *development* of the finished structure. It is here that we encounter one of the major difficulties of understanding Piaget's work. Inasmuch as no one had previously attempted the task that Piaget undertook, he was obliged to create a new vocabulary. Rather than construct neologisms, however, Piaget has done two things: first he has used existing words with slightly modified meanings; and, secondly, he has used the technical vocabulary of symbolic logic. His reason for employing symbolic logic is that the language of this discipline provides a very good way of describing the structure of the intellect, just as Euclidean geometry is ideal for describing plane surfaces, and Riemannian geometry for spheres.

Instead of beginning with a long exposition of the Piagetian vocabulary, we shall try to show the *need* for the many terms that Piaget uses, and then show how the terms meet those needs. The first term for which we shall do this is one that is well known in psychology, namely "schema".

Let us start by considering our fingers.

It is fairly easy to say what the fingers are, but can we say where they begin (or end, depending on which way we look at them)? The knuckles provide a convenient demarcation point, but there is no real line at which the fingers end and the hand begins. The same is true of the hand and wrist, the wrist and forearm, and indeed every bodily structure. Despite the difficulty over boundaries, we can and do talk of parts of the body as distinct.

What we have been saying of structure goes also (though less obviously) for function. The body has a number of systems (digestive, respiratory, circulatory, and so on), but it nevertheless functions as a whole: if one of the systems is damaged, the whole body is affected. Nevertheless, it is convenient to talk of the systems as if they were separate.

What is true of the structure and functions of the body is true of the intellect. For instance, the neonate at first sucks only when put to the breast, but soon begins to show searching behaviour when picked up by his mother at feeding time. This behaviour is different from the action of reaching for objects just outside the baby's grasp. It is convenient to have a word for an organized set of actions, and the word Piaget chooses is "schema".*

Just as bodily structures grow and develop with maturity and use, so do schemata. For instance, once a child knows how to pick up his toy bricks he will be able to pick up (or at least try to pick up) lumps of coal, milk bottles, and kittens. Piaget describes this modifiability by saying that schemata are *mobile*. This clearly distinguishes a schema from a simple stimulus–response connection: *a schema is essentially active.*

We have been talking about the behaviour of babies, and there is a very important reason for this beside the obvious one that we all start our active lives as babies. The essential characteristic of a baby's behaviour in the first 18 months of life is that it is *sensorimotor*, that is to say that, faced with a problem (for instance, how to reach an attractive plastic ring dangled above his cot) the baby *does something*. Babies aged 2 years or less seldom give

---

* In their latest work, Piaget and Inhelder (1968) reserve the word "schema" for organizations of images, and adopt the term "scheme" for organizations of actions. The usefulness of this distinction is not obvious and, in the present text, the word "scheme" is used in its customary, non-technical sense, "schema" being used in the sense given in the paragraph above.

the impression of thinking out a problem. After 2 years they do (though naturally at a very simple level). The major characteristic of mature, intelligent behaviour is thinking out a problem before acting. Often an adult does not need to act at all: when he has solved an anagram, for instance, he may simply grunt, turn over, and go to sleep. In other words, an intelligent, mature individual can solve problems in his head. Yet he had to start, as a baby, by actually doing things. Therefore his actions must have become internalized. Piaget's approach to intelligence is to study the process of internalization from its beginning (at 2 years) to its completion (at about 12 years). Piaget's term for an internalized action is an *operation*, so, for Piaget, the development of the intellect consists in the growth of operational thinking.

The term "operation" is important in another connection. In 1927 Bridgman introduced to science the idea of "operational definition", that is to say, the idea that we should define our concepts in terms of the actual operations that we carry out in order to exemplify them; for instance, we might define electricity in terms of deposition of silver at one pole of an electrolyte, the deflection of a galvanometer needle, the rise of temperature in a wire along which a current is passed, and so on. Clearly, when stated as baldly as this, there are obvious deficiencies in operational definitions, and many words have been devoted to discussing whether, or to what extent, definitions (in psychology, or any other science) can or should be operational. Nevertheless, the idea has been very valuable in clarifying certain aspects of scientific thinking, and bears a very interesting relationship to the philosophical school of "logical positivism", which held that the meaning of a proposition is the way in which we verify it; for example, what I mean by "there is a chair on the other side of that door" is that, if I walked through that door I should see a chair. If I did not see a chair, the proposition would have been wrong, but there is only one way to test the meaning of such a proposition, and that is *by doing something*. When we remember that, for Piaget, every thought was once an action, we see a possible link between contemporary psychology and contemporary philosophy. As Piaget (1953) says: "operationalism provides real ground on which logic* and psychology can meet . . . operations are actual psychological activities, and all effective knowledge is based on such a system of operations."

Inasmuch as development—for Piaget—consists in the growth of operational thinking, it is convenient to adopt a teleological approach to the exposition of Piaget's work, that is to say we shall first describe the structure of the mature intellect and then review development from the perspective of maturity.

In order to understand what is involved in mature thinking, let us see what the adolescent can do that the child of 8 or 9 years cannot. A piece of wood floats, whereas a piece of iron of identical dimensions sinks. If we ask an adolescent to explain this, he will give an explanation in terms of density. He may not have learnt this concept, and his explanation may be insufficiently articulate; for instance, he may say "size for size the iron is heavier than the wood, and is too heavy to float". The essential part of the explanation lies in the qualification "size for size". A 9-year-old would be more likely to say simply "the iron is heavier". Basically this is correct, but, when he is shown a piece of wood that is demonstrably heavier than the iron, and when he sees that this floats, he is unable to qualify his answer correctly: he will continue to say that the iron is heavier, possibly adding that the large piece of wood is only heavier when it is not in the water.

The essential difference between the adolescent and the child is that the adolescent has *formalized* his answer by abstracting the appropriate physical quality from the materials and applying this to the solution of the problem. The child has been too closely tied to the *concrete situation*. Both child and adolescent have given answers in terms of operations, that is to say they have referred to relative weights, showing that they understand what is involved in the action of balancing. Piaget describes the child as at the

---

* Remember that A. J. Ayer has maintained that philosophy is a branch of logic rather than vice versa (Ayer, 1946). However, this connection between psychology and philosophy must not be pushed too far, as Piaget is severely critical of logical positivism. The suggestion is primarily heuristic in nature.

level of *concrete operations*, the adolescent at the level of *formal operations*.

As a beginning, therefore, we may offer the following developmental plan:

> Sensorimotor actions
> Operational thinking: concrete operations
>   formal operations

As it stands, however, this plan is incomplete, for the period of concrete operations is a long one, and involves the preparation for their use, because naturally the young child does not pass suddenly from sensorimotor behaviour to concrete operational thinking. For some years he appears to solve problems by a kind of intuition.

To illustrate this let us consider a specimen of social behaviour. In order to play co-operatively, a child must appreciate that other children have rights in the game, but children can play co-operatively about a year before they are able to express any realization of the fact that other people have rights. On a simpler level, a child will know that turning the pedals makes a cycle go long before he can give any sort of explanation of why this is. In other words, the child has an elementary *intuitive* conception of how things work and how he should behave.

Before this period of his life, however, the child passes through a period of exploration of the world around him. The first 2 years of life are what we may describe as "autistic", that is to say, the child's attention is directed primarily towards himself and to things only in so far as they relate to himself. The third and fourth years are devoted to the exploration of the world that is a necessary preliminary to the development of intuitive conceptions. We must note, however, that whilst it is necessary, it is not *sufficient*. As we shall see later, no amount of experience is sufficient to enable a child to pass from one developmental period to another if he is not ready. Precisely what maturational factors are involved in this readiness no one is, as yet, able to say.

We may now write out a more complete developmental plan,

indicating roughly the ages to which the various periods correspond.

I	Sensorimotor phase	0–2 years
II*	Pre-operational phase:	
	1. Preconceptual stage	2–4 years
	2. Stage of intuitive thought	4–7 years
III	Concrete operations phase	7–11½ years
IV	Formal operations phase	11½ years onwards

The sensorimotor phase deserves more detailed consideration than we have given it so far because a very great deal happens in the first 2 years of life. As we know, the baby learns to walk, talk, feed himself, and keep clean in the matter of elimination. In a period of 2 years, in which the essential preliminaries of socialization are established, we should expect a study to reveal a detailed process of growth. In Piaget's scheme it is usual to distinguish six stages in the sensorimotor phase. Different translators render the names of these steps differently, and the following terms and brief descriptions (which will be expanded later) are intended as brief identifications: the ages in months show approximately when one can expect the different steps to appear.

1. Random and reflex action	0–1 month
2. Primary circular reactions, with the first appearance of schemata	1–4 months
3. Secondary circular reactions, with the appearance of procedures designed to cause the continuation of interesting sights	4–8 months
4. Co-ordination of secondary schemata and their application to new situations	8–12 months
5. Tertiary circular reactions, with the invention of new means to gain desired ends	12–18 months

* Some commentators link II and III together under the heading "Phase of preparation for, and use of concrete operations", but this seems unnecessarily cumbersome.

6. Invention of new means, by mental combinations rather than actions, that is to say the appearance of elementary memory and planning   18–24 months

It is interesting to observe that the appearance of elementary memory and planning coincides with the child's instrumental use of language. Most children speak their first word at about a year, and in the second year of life they employ their language to structure their environment (by naming objects) and to modify it (by asking for things). Luria (1961) has shown how even very young children can solve problems that are initially too difficult for them if an adult shows them how to use their language to solve the problems.

In the next few pages we shall give a brief description of the different sorts of behaviour that can be expected at various periods of development. Before we do, however, we must explain a few more technical terms. We mentioned earlier that experience is necessary for development but not sufficient. We also said that schemata are essentially active. These statements, taken together, imply that development is a process of interaction between organism and environment. We need terms to describe this interaction.

Let us first realize that at each period of development the intellect is *organized* (into schemata). Because it is organized it is *adapted* to the environment. However, as we have seen, schemata are mobile, so adaptation is essentially an active process. Let us think for a moment about the process of digestion. Food must be modified by the body in order that the body may use it; however, as we grow older, we consume different foodstuffs —first milk, then baby foods, and finally solids. In other words, in order that the digestive system may *assimilate* new foodstuffs it must *accommodate* itself to them. Piaget regards the intellect as functioning in much the same way, so we may represent the relationship between organism and environment as follows:

Because of the intellect's *organization*
it exhibits   *adaptation*, a two-way process comprising
                                   accommodation   and
                                   assimilation

We may take, as a psychological example, the case of infant feeding that we have already mentioned. The neonate sucks when put to the breast, and (as we know from studies of Freud) his mouth becomes the focus of his pleasurable sensations. The fact that his sensations have a focus means that the primordial "booming, buzzing confusion" is becoming organized. That is to say, by assimilating a feature of the world (the breast) his intellect has to a certain extent accommodated itself to that world. The infant is now in a position to assimilate other features of the world, for example his mother's face. His intellect is now more structured than it was before, which is another way of saying that it has further accommodated itself to environmental demands, and so is in a position to assimilate more.

When the environment requires the schema to accommodate in order to assimilate new features, the schema is obviously developing, just as the body develops by taking in new foodstuffs. By analogy with digestion, Piaget describes an experience requiring accommodation as an *aliment*.

We have now sketched the outline of Piaget's work, and are in a position to describe the essential features of each period of development. The descriptions will be relatively brief, for two main reasons. In the first place, the major aim of this book is not to describe what Piaget has done but to explain why he has done it. In the second, many commentators have given long, detailed descriptions of Piaget's developmental studies, the most recent being Baldwin (1967) and Flavell (1963), and this book is not intended to compete with theirs. Students who are interested in Piaget's developmental studies will find it helpful to consult these other commentaries for more detail before, of course, turning to Piaget's own works.

CHAPTER 3

The Sensorimotor Phase and
Pre-operational Thinking

WE HAVE seen that Piaget's main concern is with the development of intelligence, that is to say, with the growth of operational thinking. However, in addition to his works specifically on this topic (e.g. *The Psychology of Intelligence* and *The Origin of Intelligence in the Child*) Piaget has published studies of what Kant (following Aristotle) called the intellectual "categories", that is the forms under which our experience of the world is organized. Piaget has also produced a study of the growth of moral understanding as well as studies of imagery, perception, and so on.

If one examines the child's understanding of his physical and social environment, one frequently observes similar cognitive structures occurring at different ages. Suppose we take a piece of plasticine and in the presence of a 4-year-old roll it into a sausage shape and ask if there is more plasticine now that it is rolled thin then when it was in the form of a round ball. Most 4-year-olds will say either that there is more (because it is longer) or less (because it is thinner). Suppose we chop up the plasticine into six pieces and put the pieces in one pan of a balance, putting a weight in the other pan to balance the plasticine. In the child's presence we remove the plasticine, chop it into twelve pieces, and ask if the twelve pieces will weigh more than the six. The average 4-year-old will say either that they weigh more (because there are more pieces) or that they weigh less (because the pieces are smaller). If we repeated these experiments with an 8-year-old, the child would tell us that the plasticine retains the same quantity and weight throughout. At some time in the intuitive stage, therefore, the child grasps the notion of the permanence of quantity of matter and of weight. Typically, however, the understanding of permanence of quantity develops before that of permanence of weight. What we see here is a temporal gap, or *décalage*. Because this gap nevertheless occurs within the limits of one stage of development, Piaget describes it as a *horizontal décalage*.

Another sort of *décalage* is crucial to the whole process of development. We have seen that the child's intellect is always organized but that it is organized in different ways at different ages. At first it is organized in sensorimotor terms, later in concrete operational terms, and, finally, in formal operational terms. Thus a 9-year-old will be able to solve problems involving serial ordering only if given the appropriate materials to exemplify the problems; but a 12-year-old will be able to solve problems stated as follows: "John is taller than Jane, who is shorter than Bill, but taller than Dick. Who is the next tallest after John?" Basically the same problems can be solved, but children solve them in different ways according to the stage or phase that they have attained. Piaget describes this sort of temporal gap as a *vertical décalage*.

Whereas the idea of horizontal *décalage* points out the danger of regarding intellectual performance at any one stage as *homogeneous*, the notion of vertical *décalage* warns us not to regard intellectual activity at different stages as too *heterogeneous*. Moreover, the existence of these *décalages* poses a fundamental problem for anyone who tries to expound development stage by stage. Inevitably there will appear to be gaps at certain parts of the exposition and repetitions at others. Furthermore the sheer volume of Piaget's investigations means that one must write at very great length in order to give a truly adequate account, so that the reader is likely to lose sight of the wood because of the number and variety of trees. Since this book is intended to be a map of the woods rather than a flora, our account of Piaget's findings must not be regarded as a substitute for the fuller commentaries.

The Sensorimotor Phase

The baby, building on his neonatal reflexes, learns to co-ordinate his sensorimotor activities and to exercise a primitive control over his environment. By the age of 2 he will have learnt to recognize the limits of his own body and to recognize the more or less permanent existence of objects apart from himself. Furthermore, as a result of his kicking and arm-waving, in the course of which he must frequently have knocked things over, he will have developed an elementary understanding of cause and effect, and a limited power to do things intentionally.

From the start of life we see, more or less clearly, the working of accommodation and assimilation. With regard to accommodation, for example, the infant rapidly shows progress in the skill of locating the nipple before sucking. That is to say, whereas at first the neonate sucks when put to the breast, later he sucks only after locating the nipple. In other words, the stimuli necessary to start the action change with experience. Furthermore, we know that the strength and efficiency of sucking improve with experience, which suggests that practice is necessary for the effective maintenance of the reflex. However, the signs of accommodation and assimilation are not readily distinguishable at this stage, and it is better to regard them as *precursors* of what will become clear at later stages.

In addition to accommodation, of course, we observe assimilation. Piaget distinguishes four types of assimilation, and, although the differences between them do not become clear until later, they are presaged in the first month. They are as follows.

i. *Reproductive (or Functional) Assimilation.* In terms of classical educational theory, reproductive assimilation is the strengthening of stimulus–response connections through exercise. As applied to the feeding situation, we find that the action of sucking, being pleasurable in itself, induces further sucking. This leads us to recognize an important element in Piaget's theory, namely that the exercise of schemata is *inherently satisfying;* in this, of course, Piaget differs from most motivational theorists, who would regard satisfaction as resulting only from the reduction of needs.

ii. *Generalizing Assimilation.* We have just mentioned that Piaget regards the exercise of schemata as inherently satisfying. This implies that the completion of a response pattern becomes the stimulus for the repetition of the response. For instance the child sucks from the breast, then swallows the milk. He is unable to suck whilst swallowing, but after he has swallowed, he responds to the continued tactile stimulation of his lips and mouth by swallowing again. In this way a *circular reaction* is set up. In the repetition of a circular reaction, the child does not always come into contact with precisely the same object each time. In sucking, for instance, he comes to learn that he can also suck his thumb, and (later) the teat of a feeding bottle.

iii. *Recognitory Assimilation.* The difference between the thumb and a bottle-teat is, of course, that the latter is nourishing whereas the former is not. When he is hungry, therefore, sucking his thumb will not satisfy. The infant shows that he recognizes and discriminates objects by behaving towards them differently in different circumstances.

iv. *Reciprocal Assimilation.* This is not a distinct form of assimilation, but refers to the co-ordination of schemata, a co-ordination that occurs when schemata assimilate each other. For instance, a child may learn a visual schema, that is to say may learn how visually to inspect an object, and may separately learn a manipulative schema, that is, how to handle an object. Eventually the child will learn to look in order to handle, and handle in order to obtain a better view of the object. This reciprocal assimilation of schemata contributes eventually to the development of the understanding of the nature of objects.

1. *Stage of random and reflex action*

The neonate's behaviour is almost completely autistic, and his intermittent contacts with external reality (mainly at feeding time) do not essentially affect the automatic, largely undirected use of reflexes.

2. *Stage of primary circular reactions*

We have already explained that a "circular reaction" is one in which the completion of a response pattern is the stimulus for its repetition. By "primary" Piaget means that the first circular reactions to appear are part of the baby's innate behavioural repertoire, for instance sucking and grasping. What is characteristic of this stage is that the baby is no longer responding in a purely reflex manner, but his behaviour shows the rudiments of voluntary action. At this stage, therefore, we see the operation of recognitory assimilation, and this stage marks the start of the growth of schemata.

Although the baby's actions are voluntary, they cannot be described as purposive. His voluntary actions serve to prolong the reflex patterns of the first stage. For instance, if an infant is taken away from the breast whilst he is still hungry, he will try to move his head back to the direction of the breast. It is still too early in his development, however, for us to say that he is doing this *in order* to get more milk.

The baby's voluntary actions, be they grasping, groping, sucking, or merely looking and listening, bring him into contact with new objects, so we see generalizing assimilation at this stage. Inasmuch as a response to new objects may entail slightly modified behaviour on the baby's part, we see the possibility of distinguishing assimilation and accommodation, which it was impossible to distinguish in the reflex stage. The distinction is minimal in stage 2, but becomes more pronounced in later stages.

3. *Stage of secondary circular reactions*

The major difference between a primary and a secondary circular reaction is that the secondary circular reaction is directed more to surrounding objects, whereas the primary circular reaction is directed almost exclusively to the child's own body. If a baby observes that moving his legs is followed by movement of toys suspended above his cot, he will continue to move his legs to ensure the continuation of this interesting spectacle. We cannot say that the child appreciates the casual connection, because a similar result is observed if the connection is artificially set up by an adult experimenter, for instance if the experimenter brings a toy into the child's view when the child performs an arbitrarily chosen action. Removal of the toy will be followed by a repetition of the movement on the child's part. We can talk of these actions as "secondary" because the movements involved are not the instinctive ones such as sucking or grasping.

Once a baby has developed a schema involving an action and the appearance of a favoured object, he may employ the same action in connection with other favoured objects. His behaviour thus generalizes, and we see the beginnings of *intentional* behaviour. This is made possible because, by now, the baby is gaining a fair degree of control over his visual-motor co-ordination, that is to say, if he wants to grasp something out of his reach, he is able to direct his hand towards the object with a good measure of success.

Of course, a baby will sometimes behave in a way that indicates that he wants something out of reach, or that he wants a parent to continue doing something that is interesting to him, even though his parent is some distance away. The nature of the baby's action reveals a fundamental lack of understanding of the cause–effect relation, and indeed we cannot expect such an understanding before 6 or 7 years.

It is important to note that the behaviour directed towards attaining a desired object, or prolonging an interesting spectacle, characteristically occurs immediately after the object or spectacle has been shown and then removed. The child does not behave, in the absence of the object or entertainment, as if he wants it to appear. This restriction sets a definite limitation on the intentionality mentioned earlier. However it clearly shows that the baby has some understanding of the permanence of objects and the stability of the world.

A very interesting characteristic of this stage is what may be called *motor recognition*. Let us consider a baby who has developed a secondary circular reaction in connection with certain familiar objects. If these objects are now presented out of reach the baby may carry out the movements of the secondary circular reaction in a rudimentary form. Observations suggest that the baby is not attempting to reach the objects, but is performing the movements that, for him, define the object. This may be the beginning of the process of internalization, whereby overt actions eventually give place to contemplative thought.

Finally, an important characteristic of this stage is the clear appearance of imitation. Although younger infants may appear to imitate (for instance one will start crying when another starts), it is not before this stage that we can be sure that the child is imitating. For example, a baby of this age will clench and unclench his hand in imitation of an adult. An important restriction of the baby's power of imitation is that he can only imitate by means of those of his own actions that he can observe: he cannot, for instance, put out his tongue in imitation of an adult, because he cannot see his own tongue.

4. *Stage of co-ordination of secondary schemata*

The essential characteristic of this stage is the advance in intentional behaviour. Whereas in stage 3 this is limited, in so far as the child performs certain actions to cause the reappearance of a favourite object or event (and, moreover, displays behaviour that, rationally speaking, is irrelevant to the desired end), in stage 4 we can observe the child directing his behaviour towards a desired outcome. For instance, he will push away obstacles between himself and his goal, and the pushing away will not simply occur in the course of his reaching for the object, but will clearly be done for the purpose of reaching the goal; or, if he sees an adult's hand cause an interesting movement in an object, he will attempt to move the adult's hand in order to bring about the desired movement. Clearly what has happened is that the secondary circular reactions have become differentiated, with the means subordinated to the end, whereas previously the end and the means formed part of one secondary reaction. We may therefore talk of the establishment and co-ordination of secondary schemata, as the schema of pushing is employed in order to make possible the schema of grasping.

The baby's perceptual world now shows a simple organization: the fact that he removes obstacles to reach desired objects shows that the baby understands that some things are spatially in front of others. The organization is revealed in another way, too, namely in the child's recognition that some events "stand for" others; for instance the baby will expect to find fruit juice in a spoon taken from a tin that habitually yields fruit juice, and will show disappointment if the expectation is not fulfilled. Clearly such anticipation would not be possible if the child had not learned that some events occur before others.

The child's powers of imitation are increased at this stage, and he can imitate even if he cannot observe his own actions; for example, he can make grimaces in imitation of an adult.

What we are witnessing at this stage is a growth in the child's emancipation from individual situations and his ability to apply his schemata to new events. However, we must not exaggerate the baby's new-found freedom. If a doll is hidden behind a cushion, the baby can push aside the cushion in order to obtain it; but if, after he has done this a number of times we remove the doll on the next occasion, and in the baby's full view, place it behind another cushion, he will look behind the *first* cushion. It is as if his habit of repeating a previously successful action is too strong to be overcome in the new circumstances.

5. *Stage of tertiary circular reactions*

In stage 4 we have observed the child differentiating actions into means and ends. In stage 5 he discovers new means. Let us suppose that his normal action of pushing does not enable him to attain his object, but that in trying to push away the obstacle he *pulls* it away instead. He has discovered a new means, and naturally he will repeat the action on future occasions, so this novel reaction becomes circular. What is distinct about his behaviour in this stage is that he will *vary* his actions, thus trying out new movements rather than simply repeating actions that he has discovered. This is why Piaget calls the reactions *tertiary* rather than secondary.

Babies at this stage of development spend a considerable amount of time exploring new objects and investigating to see what can be done with them. In this way the infant not only discovers new means of achieving desired ends, he also starts to obtain a clearer understanding of the nature of objects, and the relationships of objects with each other and with his body. The type of error described at the end of our account of stage 4 is no longer made, because the child now searches where he saw the object disappear, even if this involves making a movement not previously made. However, he is not capable of reasoning about hidden movements, and if an adult puts an object behind an obstacle then surreptitiously moves it, the child will display incomprehension when he does not find the object. In stage 6 he will be able to employ a mental representation of the world to help him solve problems.

The baby's powers of imitation are more advanced now than in earlier stages. For instance, Piaget describes how his daughter, after watching her father swing his watch on its chain then put it in front of her, picked it up and tried to swing it herself. At first she made the mistake of holding the chain too near the watch, so she put it down, then picked it up again in such a way as to have a greater length of chain.

The baby's attempts at imitating his parents constitute one way in which he learns about himself and about the world. Another way is play, although play at this stage serves primarily to amuse the child, and so Piaget terms it *ludic* play. Play may be theoretically distinguished from imitation because, in Piagetian terms, imitation is essentially accommodation, whereas play (as we shall see in our discussion of stage 6) is essentially assimilation. To put it another way, in imitation the baby behaves as if he were someone else, thus accommodating himself; in play the baby treats different objects in intrinsically the same way, thus assimilating new objects to existing schemata. In practice the distinction is not easily made, as children often imitate for fun.

6. *Stage of invention of new means through mental combinations*

The great advance of this stage is the baby's powers of representing the world by mental images or (to use Tolman's term) by "cognitive maps". This is shown in a number of ways. For instance, if the direct path to a child's goal is blocked, he will take another route; this indicates that the baby now has a mental representation of the world around him *and of his place in it*, in other words he can now look upon himself as an object among other objects. If a ball is rolled behind some furniture, the baby will now go to where the ball can be expected to reappear, even if the furniture is so arranged that this entails his initially going in the opposite direction from his goal. The baby's behaviour is now showing a clear emancipation from sensorimotor connections.

Just as the baby is no longer restricted by spatial connections, so he is relatively freed from temporal linkages. For example, Piaget's daughter one day observed a young visitor screaming and stamping with such vigour that he moved his playpen; *the next day*, in the absence of the visitor, the little girl tried this for herself, and the nature of her screaming and stamping was such as to make it obvious that she was experimenting in an attempt to move her own playpen. This form of imitative behaviour (which Piaget calls *deferred imitation*) is a great advance on what has gone before, because it takes place in the absence of the model.

The power of mental representation makes it possible for the baby in the second year of life to show what we customarily term "insight". Piaget describes how one young baby tried to put a watch chain into a matchbox link by link, and inevitably failed because the weight of the chain pulled it out again. A slightly older baby, after initial failure, rolled up the chain and put it into the matchbox in this way. The appearance of the correct solution did not come accidentally, but showed the

suddenness that is familiar to us from such studies of insight as
Köhler's work with chimpanzees. In Piaget's terms, we are
witnessing the invention of new means through reciprocal
assimilation of schemata, which takes place *mentally* rather than
overtly.

There is, nevertheless, an important link with overt action.
Piaget describes how his baby daughter, being unable to retrieve
an object from a box because the opening was too small, opened
her mouth wide in imitation of the opening of the box. It was as
if, being unable to use words to represent the problem to herself,
she was employing a simple motor action as a *symbol* of the result
she wished to achieve. We are witnessing here the beginning of
the use of symbolization in problem solving, which will become of
much greater importance with the developing use of language in
the next stage.

The advance that we have observed in the power of representation makes possible a change in the nature of play. Earlier the
child's play consisted of repeating, for his own satisfaction, actions
that gave him pleasure. At stage 6 the child can behave *as if*
he were performing a pleasurable action, for instance rubbing his
dry hands together and pretending that he is washing them;
or treating objects as if they were something else, for example
using a table cloth like a pillow. Thus the child is no longer
interested merely in *identity;* at this stage *similarity* is of interest,
which means that the baby is abstracting and comparing common
properties of different objects. In this way, as the ability to play
develops, it becomes an important element in the child's capacity
for understanding, and coming to terms with, the surrounding
world.

To summarize this phase of development we may say that the
first stage consists of reflexes, then follows a stage in which actions
made reflexly are repeated, and non-reflex actions are discovered.
Next comes a stage in which these newly discovered non-reflex
actions are repeated, and then they become co-ordinated and
actively directed. Finally comes the ability to represent the world

internally and to think out the solutions to simple problems before acting. This development is accompanied and assisted by play, which often takes the form of imitation, although imitation may be employed in its own right to solve problems. By the end of this phase the baby has a much clearer understanding of objects and his relationships with them which means that his initial autism (treating things as if they were virtually extensions of himself) has largely broken down, and he is ready to use his newly developed powers of symbolization and elementary reasoning to gain a clearer understanding of the world, which is the function of the next phase of development. Nevertheless, the child still looks on things from the point of view of their relations with himself, that is to say, he shows a marked degree of *egocentricity*.

The Pre-operational Phase

The pre-operational phase comprises the child's development from the close of the sensorimotor phase up to the time when his thought becomes operational (in Piaget's technical sense of this term). The child is beginning to take an interest in the people and things around him, though essentially from his point of view rather than theirs, and this egocentrism is characteristic of this phase of development. The child believes, for instance, that everyone has the same view of things as himself and (to take a specific example) if he is seated at one side of a table, in the middle of which is a model showing houses and hills, and an experimenter is seated at the other side, the child will be unable to make a drawing of what the model will look like to the experimenter. A hill may cut off the view of a house from the experimenter's side of the table, but as long as the child can see the house he believes that everyone else will also be able to see it. Of course, the child's understanding of relationships and points of view improves as he grows older and becomes less egocentric, and it is this increase in understanding that we observe in the pre-operational phase.

The egocentrism of this phase is an intermediate step between the autism of the sensorimotor phase and fully intelligent understanding. To make the progression the child requires play and imitation, as before, and also the use of language, which develops rapidly in the pre-school period and the early school years.

It is usual to divide this phase into two stages, the preconceptual stage (from 2 to 4 years) and the stage of intuitive thinking (from 4 to 7 years); of these, the latter is richer in its yield of data.

1. *The preconceptual stage*

If we consult any psychology text for information about forming concepts we learn that concept formation involves abstracting similar features from dissimilar situations, and then generalizing

FIG. 3.1. A transductive selection of "four objects that are alike".

from particular situations to the general case. One term that covers the two aspects of abstracting and generalizing is *induction*. Induction is usually opposed to *deduction*, which is essentially the drawing of conclusions about specific instances from an understanding of the general case. In the child of 2 or 3 years we observe neither induction nor deduction, but a third activity, which Piaget calls *transduction*: transduction refers to the young child's tendency to link together any neighbouring events on the basis of what individual instances have in common. For instance, let us suppose that a 3-year-old was given a box containing a large number of wooden shapes, including red squares; some circles, half of which were red and the other half blue; and blue triangles, and was asked to give the experimenter four that were alike. The sort of solution of this problem we could expect is shown in Fig. 3.1.

This sort of solution could arise because the child links 1 and 2 by colour, 2 and 3 by shape, but 3 and 4 by colour once more. No overall common property has been abstracted, and the selection has been in terms of properties shared by adjacent instances of the event in question. (Needless to say this is not the only possible arrangement we could obtain from a child; a 3-year-old might give a satisfactory answer, but he would be wrong as often as he was right.)

A child operating on the principle of transduction will clearly not be able to form concepts, as he is tied too closely to the perceptual aspects of individual situations. Nevertheless, the child does have some general ideas, and Piaget calls these *preconcepts*. As an example of a preconcept, Piaget tells us how his young daughter saw a slug when she was on a walk with her father. A little further on she saw another slug and said "There's the slug again". When her father asked her if it were the same slug she replied that it was, but when he took her back a few yards to show her the first slug again, she continued to maintain that it was the same slug. Her father further asked "Is it another one?" and she replied "Yes". Clearly the questions were meaningless to her. It seems that she was trying to express the fact that the second slug was not the same as the first, but was unable to express the idea of "another *of the same type*". Thus she was using the word "slug" to refer neither to specific slugs nor to the class of "slugs in general" (for she had not yet developed this concept) but in what we may call a "semi-generic" way. This way of thinking about things is intermediate between references to specific individuals and genuine understanding of classes; this is why Piaget calls it a preconcept.

The inability to construct classes, and to handle the idea of class inclusion, leads the child to make errors of the type described in Piaget's well-known example of the brown and white beads. The child is given a box of wooden beads, most of which are brown, the rest white. He is asked if the beads are all wooden and, if he agrees, he is further asked "Are there more wooden or more brown beads?" Most children aged 3 or 4 will reply that there are more brown beads. The reason that young children give for this answer is that so few of the beads are white. In other words the child cannot form or handle the concept of a class of "wooden beads" containing the sub-classes "brown beads" and "white beads". To anticipate points that we shall make later, the class of "wooden beads" is an abstraction: the objects facing the child are, in fact, "brown wooden beads" and "white wooden beads", and the former class has more members than the latter. Solutions of problems involving "wooden beads" require an abstraction of which the child is not yet capable, and so, in answer to the question, the child concentrates on the most obvious difference between the beads, namely colour.

An interesting corollary of this inability to form genuine abstractions is the young child's confusion at seeing people in unexpected places or dressed in unfamiliar clothes. The same little girl, seeing her baby sister in a new bathing cap, demanded to know her name; when the baby's cap was removed, the little girl recognized her sister once more, and it was obvious from her manner that she was not playing a game and pretending not to recognize a well-known sibling.

How is it, though that the ability to form genuine concepts comes about? Piaget believes that the crucial factors are the development of mental imagery and the growth of the function of *signification*. The essential characteristic of signification is that the individual must recognize that a *signifier* (e.g. a gesture, an icon, or a word) is different from what it signifies (its *significate*), but nevertheless represents it. There are two kinds of signifiers, namely *signs* (which are socially shared and need bear no resemblance to their significates) and *symbols* (which are more or less private and usually bear some resemblance to what they symbolize). Piaget believes that the first signifiers develop from the child's powers of imitation. Whereas at first the imitations are external, eventually they become internal representations, so the first signifiers are symbols; we have seen the precursors of this symbol-ization in the sensorimotor phase, particularly in stage 6, and Piaget maintains that the child constructs symbols of many of his sensorimotor schemata. Just as imitation is a form of accommodation, the internal representation of the imitation also constitutes accommodation. This internal representation is, of course, what we call a "mental image", and Piaget maintains that mental images play a very important role in the thinking of young children, enabling them to anticipate recurring events and plan their actions in advance. (As we know from general psychology, the role played by imagery in the thinking of *adults* varies considerably, but imagery is, on the whole, less important in the thinking of adults than in that of children.)

We have said that, in signification, the signifier is distinguished from its significate, and that (according to Piaget) the signifier derives from accommodation. As we might expect, the significate is held to derive from assimilation, in other words, assimilation provides the schemata that incorporate the events to which, in the past, accommodation has been necessary. Now that we are dealing with mental representations rather than actual events, the child is able to represent these events to himself, just as he is able mentally to anticipate his actions with respect to them.

One consequence of mental representations is a widening of the time scale, as present data can now be assimilated to images evoking data assimilated in the past. Similarly, one can employ memory of past accommodations to guide one's actions in the present. (This widening of the time scale may not be an unalloyed advantage because it may lead to inappropriate behaviour, as we know from studies of personality. A common instance is the tendency to transpose the relationships that one has learnt in childhood dealings with parents to the other adults whom he meets in adolescence and early adulthood.)

So far we have talked about symbols. Among *signs* the most widely used by human beings are words. The young child at first has difficulty in employing words, for he finds it hard to understand that words must mean the same for everyone. The child's use of words is at first idiosyncratic, as we should expect from the egocentrism characteristic of this phase of development, and only at about 6 or 7 years does the child develop a satisfactory efficiency in communication.

Other signs include gestures, which for the most part are learned unconsciously, and more subtle actions, such as tone of voice, rate of breathing, direction of gaze, and so on, an (unconscious or conscious) understanding of which is vital for happy and effective social intercourse. Much unhappiness (in the adult world) springs from inadequate learning of these signs, but experimental psychologists are only just beginning to turn their attention to them.

2. *The stage of intuitive thinking*

As an example of the sorts of errors that children at the beginning of this stage make, let us consider the well-known example of permanence of quantity. Two glasses are filled to the same height with coloured liquid and the child is asked if they contain the same amount. Most 5-year-olds agree that they do. If the contents of one glass are then poured into a tall, narrow vase, and the child is asked whether the amounts of liquid are still the same, he will usually deny this. Similar results are obtained if a shallow but wide dish is substituted for the narrow vase, or if the contents are poured into two glasses similar to the first one, and so on. Children of 5 years or so believe that, if the quantities *look* different, they must *be* different. eight-year-olds, on the other hand, correctly affirm that the quantity remains exactly the same.

One may wonder if the younger children really know what the question means. In a sense they do not, and the sense in which it is true that they fail to grasp the meaning is a very important one. Let us recall what was said earlier (pp. 24–25) about operational definitions and meaning, and then ask ourselves what precisely is meant by saying that the quantity remains the same. What this means, in operational terms, is that if we poured the liquid back into the original vessel (taking care to spill none and ensuring that none was added), the level that it reached would be exactly what it was before. In other words, our understanding of the meaning of the question involves the possibility of reversing the action to return to our starting point. The 8-year-old child can do this (i.e. reverse the action) mentally (i.e. *operationally* in Piaget's terminology) but the 5-year-old cannot. This is why Piaget insists that the notion of *reversibility* is crucial to the development of operational thinking.

We may now ask why the 5-year-old child fails in this respect, and Piaget's answer is that he *centres* on one aspect of the situation. In our example the child centres on the height of the liquid, ignoring the width. In the early stages of such an experiment a child will maintain that the taller vessel contains more liquid "because it is taller". If we repeat the experiment, choosing successively wider vessels into which to pour the liquid, a point will be reached where the child will start to claim that the shallower vessel has more "because it is wider". This is an example of a primitive *regulation* of his thinking in which he begins to take account of compensating changes in different aspects of the phenomenon under consideration. As he grows older he comes to realize that *every* change in height is compensated by a change in width, which amounts to saying (in Piagetian terminology) that the child *decentres* his thinking, and is able to think about more than one aspect of the situation at a time. This facility makes it possible for him mentally to perform the compensating changes and see how he can return to his starting point.

The development of decentring is slow because at first the child, when he attempts to think out a problem, repeats in his head the sequence of actions that he has actually performed or seen others perform. It is probably through play, involving the manipulation of materials, assisted by his increasing facility in the use of language (which enables him to analyse what he is doing) that the child develops his understanding of reversibility; but this does not mean that intellectual development is solely a matter of environmental stimulation because the *maturation* of intellectual structures is vital in this respect. No amount of training in understanding the material world will assist the comprehension of a child who is not ready for it: on the other hand, inadequate training of a child who *is* old enough to understand may hinder his development. We touch here upon the educational implications of Piaget's work, the chief of which is that the right experiences must be given to the child at the most favourable time; in other words, that the teacher (and let us remember that the child's first teachers are his parents) must not force learning on the child, but should seek to provide the optimum conditions for his development.*

It will be clear from what has been said that the child in this stage is learning a very great deal about the physical world. Among other things he learns about number, distance, length, area, speed, time, and so on. We need not go into the details, as excellent brief summaries are available in the two books by Isaacs (1960, 1961). The general picture that emerges is of a growing freedom from the perceptual aspects of situations, and one further example will be sufficient to illustrate this point.

The child is shown two rows of beads, so arranged that the beads in the two rows are opposite each other. A 5-year-old will agree that the number of beads is the same in each row. If the beads of one row are now pushed together, or spread further apart, the child will maintain that the number of beads in the rows are no longer equal. An 8-year-old would not be influenced by the change in appearance, and would know that the spatial disposition of the beads does not affect their number.

What we have seen in this example, as in the example of the liquid and the vessels, is the development of an *invariant*. The child comes to realize that, whilst the physical appearance of things may change very greatly, some features of the situation stay the same. If we stop to consider what these invariants of the physical world are, we discover that they are abstractions. There

* Of course, many progressive educators have held this view. The point is that the implications of Piaget's work, as Isaacs (1960, 1961) has shown, are in agreement with the best teaching practice, not in conflict as is sometimes supposed. (See Chapter 8 of this book.)

are no "things" like numbers, quantity, and so on; these are concepts that we construct, which is why some philosophers of science call them *constructs*. This point, which it is easy to over-look, emphasizes once more the active nature of intellectual devel-opment, and shows us why it is impossible to teach such concepts to children before they are ready for them.†

At the beginning of this stage children are not ready for these concepts, but they nevertheless solve elementary problems. Suppose three differently coloured beads are to be strung on a wire which is fitted with an opaque sleeve into which the beads can be slid out of sight, as in Fig. 3.2. The child watches them

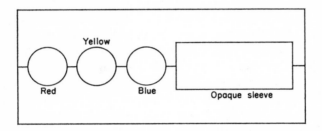

FIG. 3.2. Apparatus for studying the intuitive appreciation of the effect of rotation on the order of beads on a wire.

pushed into the sleeve and is asked the order of the colours to make sure that he has observed correctly. The frame containing the wire is rotated through 180° with the beads held inside the sleeve, in full view of the child. He is then asked which coloured bead will come out first from a specified end of the tube. Now an adult will know that an odd number of 180° rotations will reverse the order, an even number will restore it, and the colour of the middle bead will not alter. The 5-year-old child will not be able to manage this abstraction but will answer correctly for

† It seems very likely, moreover, that the formation of such concepts will be hindered until the child has developed an adequate language system. (See Chapter 9 of this book.)

one or two rotations, because he has an *intuitive* understanding of how the problem is to be solved and can picture to himself what is happening inside the sleeve. An older child grasps the idea that one turn reverses the order whilst two restore it, and can, by counting, solve the problem for a much greater number of turns. Even so, without a full understanding of the concept of odd and even numbers, he becomes confused and makes errors.

This example is an important one because it illustrates certain features of a group of transformations, and the notion of a group is crucial to Piaget's account of operational thinking: although we must treat this notion in greater detail when we discuss the phases of concrete and formal operations, it is convenient briefly to anticipate our discussion at this point. Let us picture the frame (with the beads) as mounted like a wheel. However many times it is rotated, the frame will eventually come to rest in a position that we may describe as "a position of the wheel". We can reach any position by turning the wheel clockwise or counterclockwise, and from any final position we may return to our starting point. Therefore, every action has its *inverse*. Furthermore, from any position a revolution of 360° will bring us back exactly to our starting position, so we may call a 360° turn an *identity element*. The successive positions attained by revolving a wheel are said to constitute an algebraic group, which has very important properties. Although we must defer discussion of these properties till later, we can see already how an adult's solution of the problem of the order of the beads is related to the notions of inverse and of identity element. This does not mean that an adult must understand the algebra of groups before he can solve this problem, but it does mean that an adult's thinking can be described in terms of algebraic groups, whereas the thinking of children cannot.

We have more than once referred to the increasingly important role that the child's language plays in his development. It helps him to analyse what he is doing and probably assists in concept formation (as we have already mentioned), but it also enables him to adapt to his social environment by means of conversation.

Piaget maintains that the child's speech at first contains a high proportion of egocentric reference, becoming more socially directed (or *sociocentric*) only after the age of 6 years. Many investigators have objected that Piaget exaggerates the proportion of egocentric reference in the speech of the pre-school child, but it is not our purpose at present to criticize the details of Piaget's investigations. The essential point is that the child develops an increasing ability, as he grows older, to appreciate the points of view of other people, and this is reflected in his language. The most likely situation is that the decrease in egocentric thinking and the increase in linguistic facility interact, each furthering the progress of the other. The ability to appreciate other view points means that the child learns to think in relative, rather than absolute, terms (for instance with respect to morality, justice, punishment, and so on). This means that the child of about 7 or 8 years is considerably more able than younger children to understand and deal realistically with social situations.*

Finally it must be stressed that the child's ability to reflect upon his actions (and to express these reflections in his language) characteristically develops a considerable time after these actions first appear, so that the child of 4–7 years knows how to behave in social situations (such as co-operative play), and is able to solve simple problems involving physical manipulations long before he is able to give his reasons for his behaviour or his solutions to problems. This, as we have already indicated (p. 26), is why this period of development is called the *intuitive* stage.

* The topic of language is further discussed in Chapter 9.

CHAPTER 4

Operational Thinking

LET US think of some of the things that a child aged between 7 and 11 years can be expected to do. At this time it becomes possible for the psychologist to use a wide range of intelligence test items in order to assess his development, and it is instructive to compare two of the best-known intelligence test items. On the Wechsler Intelligence Scale for Children, one item is the object-assembly in which the child is required to put various pieces together to form a meaningful whole figure. In Raven's Progressive Matrices Test, on the other hand, he chooses, from among a number of items, the one that completes a set resulting from simultaneous changes in two directions.

There is an obvious similarity between these operations, but there is also a significant difference. In the WISC object assembly the figure does not really exist until it is put together; but in the Progressive Matrices nothing is actually put together.* Raven's test demands a *logical* operation, whereas the WISC object assembly involves a spatial manipulation of material. Piaget terms the operation involved in object assembly as *infralogical*.

The child at this period of his life is developing a much clearer understanding of the nature of numbers. For instance he shows by his behaviour (even if he cannot express it) that he realizes that the meaning of $1 + 2 = 3$ is that $1 + (1 + 1) = 1 + 1 + 1$. The technical name for arriving at larger numbers by adding units is *iteration*. Iteration is also shown in multiplication when the child realizes that 4×4 means $4 + 4 + 4 + 4$. Iteration in these examples is a logical operation.

---

* Special versions, in which the items take the form of solid blocks are available, but they are an exception to the general case.

Iteration is shown in the infralogical sphere with respect to measurement. If a child is asked to construct on the floor a tower of building bricks to equal in height one constructed by the experimenter on a table, and which he is prevented from visually comparing by a screen placed in his line of sight, he shows a number of stages in the development of his ability to make his tower of the required height. These range from trying to hold his hands at the same distance apart as he walks from one tower to the other, through using his body as a measuring instrument, then using a long stick and marking off the height of the experimenter's tower. None of these methods is successful because the experimenter's tower is not built on the floor but is raised from it. The successful solution is to use a *small* stick, and see how many times it can be placed alongside the tower. Essentially this is iteration, but, as it involves manipulation of material, Piaget regards it as infralogical.

In all the examples that we have given we may observe an appreciation of reversibility. We have mentioned reversibility before, as the essential condition of solving problems involving the understanding of invariance of certain properties despite changes in others; it is in the phase of concrete operations that the notion of reversibility develops fully. It is sometimes said to "permeate" the child's thinking at this period. It is able to do this because his thinking shows an equilibrium between accommodation and assimilation.

Because an equilibrium has been reached, it is possible to offer a description of the intellect. This description must necessarily be complex and must take account of the logical and infralogical operations mentioned above, and also of the child's ability to solve certain problems (e.g., those involving class inclusion, like the brown and wooden beads, as described on p. 43). Ideally it must also account for improvements in social competence, and the child's understanding of different viewpoints (for instance that "foreignness" is relative, and that, when he goes abroad, *he* is a foreigner).

The difficulty comes with the word "ideal". What is an *ideal* description? Piaget's solution, as we have already mentioned, is to describe the intellect in terms of symbolic logic. Now symbolic logic is a kind of non-quantitative algebra, and many psychologists are prejudiced against the application to psychological material of terms and concepts drawn from such a field. Piaget regards such a prejudice as irrational. After all, he argues, psychologists use quantitative methods in statistical analysis and in test construction, so why not apply non-quantitative algebra to the description of the intellect? The justification for doing so, of course, would be that it materially assisted our purpose. Naturally, Piaget believes that it does, but it is precisely here that most people encounter the greatest stumbling block in their appreciation of Piaget. They feel that the amount of effort required to master the unfamiliar concepts is not justified in terms of the increased understanding of the intellect that would result.

The present author feels that the amount of new conceptual material that need be mastered in order to come to grips with Piaget's scheme is no greater than for the system of Clark Hull. It goes without saying that the material *could* be developed at great length and with formidable intricacies, but it can also be presented in a fairly brief and straightforward way. It is the intention of the present chapter first to offer a simplified account of Piaget's scheme, and then to indicate how this accounts for some of the complexities of the human intellect at this period of development.

Groups, Lattices and Groupings

We have already introduced the notion of a group (pp. 49–50), and we must now say more about it. A group is a set of elements having certain mathematical properties, the two most frequently quoted examples being:

(1) The successive positions of a rotating wheel, or a rigid bar rotating about its midpoint (the example that we have already given in Chapter 3).

(2) The set of positive and negative integers, including zero.

A group is defined by the following properties:

1. *Closure.* Combining any two or more elements of the set produces another member of the same set. For example, in however many ways we add and subtract positive and negative integers, we end up with a positive or negative integer or zero.

2. *Associativity.* The order in which we combine the elements does not affect the result, thus

$$(2 + 3) + 4 = 9 = 2 + (3 + 4)$$
$$(5 - 9) + 6 - 4 = -2 = 5 + 6 - 4 - 9$$

3. *General identity.* One element of the set, and one only, must be such that, when it is combined with the others, it leaves the result unchanged. This element is called the *identity element*. In the case of the rotation of a rigid bar the identity element (as we have seen, p. 50) is a rotation of 360°. In the case of integers it is 0 (zero) because adding 0 to any integer, or subtracting 0, leaves the integer unchanged.

4. *Reversibility.* For every element there is another element, called its *inverse*, which, combined with that element yields the identity element. We have seen (p. 50) that, in the case of rotations of a bar, the inverse of a rotation in one direction is an equal rotation in the other direction, bringing us back to our starting point. In the case of integers, the inverse of x is $-x$, because $x + (-x) = 0$. The inverse of $-x$ is, of course, x (because $(-x) + x = 0$). Thus $4 + (-4) = 0$, $-9 + 9 = 0$, and so on.

Now it happens that there are many mental operations that do not satisfy the criteria of a group, and Piaget calls these *groupings*. Before we can explain what a grouping is, we must explain yet another term, namely *lattice*. Happily this is more obviously connected with the child's mental activities, as it refers to classification.

The child between 7 and 11 years is very much concerned with classifying objects in the world around him. A 3-year-old may well know the word "dogs". Only later will he learn the terms "poodle", "dachshund", and "chow", and come to realize that chows, poodles, and dachshunds are subdivisions of the class of dogs. Later still he will learn that dogs, cats, horses, pigs, and cows are all mammals, and that birds and beetles, whilst they are animals, are not mammals. A classification of animals that comprehends this knowledge would look like the following:

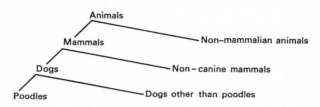

We have here the elements of a lattice, which we may represent more formally as follows:

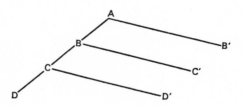

We see that B and B' are included in A; C and C' are included in B; D and D' in C.

We can say that D and D' *join* at C; C and C' *join* at B; B and B' *join* at A. We describe C as the *least upper bound* (l.u.b.) of D and D' because C is the smallest class that includes D and D'. Similarly, B is the l.u.b. of C and C'; and A is the l.u.b. of B and B'. Translating this into English, and referring to our example, we can say that "poodles" and "dogs other than poodles" join at "dogs", in other words that "dogs" is the l.u.b. of "poodles" and "dogs other than poodles". Similarly, "mammals" is the l.u.b. of "dogs" and "non-canine mammals".

Now let us ask: "What creatures are both poodles and dogs?"

The answer is, of course, "poodles". In other words, the class "dogs" and the class "poodles" *meet* at "poodles". Similarly, "mammals" and "dogs" *meet* at "dogs", because the only creatures that are both mammals and dogs are dogs. In terms of our symbols, A and B meet at B; C and D meet at D. Another way of putting this is to describe B as the *greatest lower bound* (g.l.b.) of A and B; C is the g.l.b. of B and C; D is the g.l.b. of C and D.

We may therefore define a lattice as a structure whose elements are so related that any two of them have one l.u.b. and one g.l.b.

Strictly speaking, the example that we have given is of a semi-lattice, which requires only that every two elements in a set have an l.u.b. Let us suppose that we had a classification as follows:

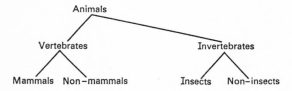

We may represent this classification formally as follows:

In this scheme, of which our first illustration is a part, every two elements have an l.u.b. For instance, the l.u.b. of G and H' is E (the smallest class that comprises mammals and insects is "animals": or one might say that "mammals" and "insects" join at "animals"). It is not the case that every two elements have a g.l.b.; for example, there is no g.l.b. of F and H because there are no creatures that are both vertebrates and insects.

Lattices as such exist only in the field of abstract symbolism, for instance truth tables of logic, and are therefore characteristic of the phase of formal operations. The phase of concrete operations is characterized by semi-lattices, which may appear to be lattices only because (as in our example) they are incomplete. However, even semi-lattices have the lattice properties that are relevant to our further discussion.

Let us look again at the notion of l.u.b. with reference to our original example. Suppose someone listed all the different types of dog in the world and then asked us to add to this the class "poodles"; we should see at once that the operation would be unnecessary and illegitimate, because the class of dogs (C in our example) includes the class of poodles D as well as that of non-poodle dogs D'. Therefore $C + D = C$.

We should obtain a similar result by adding poodles and mammals ($B + D = B$), dogs and animals ($A + C = A$), and so on. Now if $A + C = A$, $B + D = B$, $C + D = C$, and so on, we realize that every class is playing the role of an identity element with respect to the classes that are supraordinate to it. This is a special type of identity, which Piaget calls *resorption*.

Let us consider another possibility. Suppose that two people independently listed all the different types of dogs in the world. If we were given these two lists and were asked to obtain a total, we should realize once more that the task would be meaningless and unnecessary, for however many lists we had, the total number of types of dog would remain the same. In other words (to revert to symbols) $C + C = C$. Thus every class plays the role of identity element with respect to itself. This is another kind of special identity which Piaget calls *tautology*. (Tautology is clearly different from the iteration that we noted for groups. In a group $C + C$ would be $2C$.)

Groupings of Classes and Relations in the Phase of Concrete Operations

Now the structures that Piaget calls *groupings* possess the four properties of groups (closure, associatitity, general identity, and reversibility) plus the special identities (resorption and tautology) of lattices. A grouping is therefore not wholly a group (because, for example, it lacks the property of iteration), but it is more than a lattice: it has features of both lattices and groups. Piaget believes that the grouping is a significant and valuable model for intellectual operations. He distinguishes between groupings of *classes* and groupings of *relations*, listing four of each. It is at this point that any exposition of Piaget's thinking risks tying itself up in detail, so, since exposition of the main outlines is our primary aim, we shall deliberately over-simplify the presentation in the interests of clarity by not illustrating, for each grouping, the application of the five defining properties. The student may work them out for himself, or read the very full account in Flavell.*

GROUPINGS OF CLASSES

I. *Primary addition of classes*

We have already given the essence of this grouping in our explanation of what a lattice is. We can add together any number of our classes, or subtract one from others; for example, we can think of all the mammals minus all the dogs, and end with all the non-canine mammals $(B - C = C')$.

A child can be considered to display this grouping if he can solve the problem of the brown and wooden beads (see p. 43),

GROUPINGS OF RELATIONS

V. *Addition of asymmetrical relations*

An asymmetrical relation is one like "father of", because if X is the father of Y, then Y is not the father of X. A more general example would be "greater than", because if X is greater than Y, Y is not greater than X. This particular relation is said to be *transitive*, because if $X > Y$, and $Y > Z$, then $X > Z$. These relations denote *ordered differences* between terms. The child may be said to

* The numbering of the groupings here differs from Flavell's in following Piaget's later numbering rather than the earlier, which Flavell adopts.

because the problem may be represented as

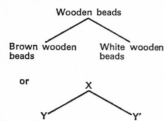

Wooden beads

Brown wooden beads   White wooden beads

or

X

Y'   Y'

The solution may be described as an appreciation of the fact of class inclusion, or that $X = Y + Y'$.

II. *Secondary addition of classes (Vicariances)*

Let us return to our example of the dogs. We have written:

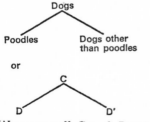

Dogs

Poodles   Dogs other than poodles

or

C

D   D'

We may call C and D *primary* classes, and D' a *secondary* class. It would be possible to subdivide the secondary class as follows:

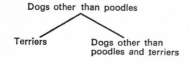

Dogs other than poodles

Terriers   Dogs other than poodles and terriers

exhibit this grouping if he can solve problems involving *seriation*, for instance, arranging a number of sticks in order of size, then inserting another set in the appropriate spaces between the first sticks. Seriation involves viewing each element (except the extremes) in relation to *two* others simultaneously, and seeing not only that $Y > X$, but also that $Y < Z$.

VI. *Addition of symmetrical relations*

A good example of a symmetrical relation is "brother of", because if X is the brother of Y, then Y is the brother of X. It is clear that if X is the brother of Y, and Y is the brother of Z, then X is the brother of Z. We may symbolize this relationship as $\leftrightarrow$, thus if $X \leftrightarrow Y$ and $Y \leftrightarrow Z$, then $X \leftrightarrow Z$.

A child may be considered as showing this grouping when he shows, by his behaviour and language that he grasps the full significance of relations such as brother, foreigner, and so on.

In terms of symbols we have:

The pattern that is emerging is that unprimed letters C, D, E refer to specified classes (dogs, poodles, and terriers respectively), whereas primed letters D', E' refer to their complementary classes, or remainders ("dogs other than poodles" and "dogs other than poodles or terriers" respectively). We might continue to subdivide the primed classes, for instance E' could be divided into F (chows) and F' (dogs other than poodles, terriers, or chows). In this way we should obtain a hierarchy of series—primary, secondary, tertiary, and so on.

However, we see that "chows" plus "dogs other than poodles, terriers, or chows", equals "dogs" $(F + F' = C)$. Similarly, "terriers" plus "dogs other than terriers or poodles" equals "dogs"; and "poodles" plus "dogs other than poodles" equals "dogs" $(E + E' = C;$ $D + D' = C)$. In other words, in equations involving C, we may substitute $D + D'$, $E + E'$, or $F + F'$, because each of these logical sums equals C. Piaget describes these as *complementary substitutions* or *vicariances*.

A child may be said to exhibit this grouping when he realizes that he may classify a collection of objects in different ways.

III. *Co-univocal (one-to-many) multiplication of classes*

Let us imagine that we are investigating degrees of family relationship among the male descendants of a man to the third filial generation. All his sons would be brothers, but among his grandsons there would be some who are brothers, whilst others might be first cousins. It would not matter for our purposes if there were no cousins (if, for instance, only the eldest son in each generation fathered any children): the point is that such degrees of relationship are possible. We could set up a matrix of relationships as follows, in order to record the numbers in each category.

VII. *Co-univocal (one-to-many) multiplication of relations*

In grouping III we were concerned to represent members of a family falling into different numbers of classes (sons of X and brother of each other, etc.). Suppose we now consider relationships as such, and ask "If X is the brother of Y who is the father of Z, what is the relationship of X to Z?" The answer is, of course, "uncle". So "brother of the father of" equals "uncle of". This is a simple example, but one may easily become confused, as the well-known couplet

Brothers and sisters have I none,

But that man's father is my father's son

	Sons of X	Grand- sons of X	Great- grand- sons of X
Brothers	+	+	+
First cousins	−	+	+
Second cousins	−	−	+

The cells marked + may or may not contain members, but membership of these cells is possible. It is not possible for any individuals to belong in cells marked—(none of a man's sons can be other than brothers of each other, and none of his grandsons can be second cousins of each other, and so on).

We have taken an example of family relationships, but our interest is not in the relationships as such, but in classification and, in particular, the different classes that may be established by one-to-many correspondences among classes (e.g. the correspondence of "grandsons of X" to the classes "brothers", "first cousins", and "second cousins"). We may say that the child displays this grouping when he understands the principle of one-to-many correspondence among classes.

testifies. The problem here is to elucidate the relationship "son of the son of the father of". By multiplying together various degrees of relationship (for instance, "grandfather of the first cousin of the second cousin of") one may generate all possible degrees of family relationship.

Of course *family* relationships are not the only types of relations to which this grouping (or grouping III) applies, but it is convenient to take them as an example because they are so familiar to us. We may say that the child shows this grouping when he understands the principle of one-to-many correspondences among relationships.

IV. *Bi-univocal (one-to-many) multiplication of classes*

Suppose that we take a class and divide it in two different ways. For instance, we may divide the class of animals into vertebrates and invertebrates. We may alternatively divide it into creatures that fly and creatures that do not fly. We have

	Flying	Non-flying
Vertebrates	Flying verte-brates	Non-flying verte-brates
Inverte-brates	Flying inverte-brates	Non-flying inverte-brates

Thus we generate a square matrix formed by multiplying classes across and down. The classes down have been set in a one-to-one correspondence with the classes across. We should note that the result of multiplying two classes in this way is always and necessarily to obtain a smaller class.

Essentially this is the grouping involved in the solution of simpler problems of the matrix type, for instance, a child

VIII. *Bi-univocal (one-to-one) multiplication of relations*

Imagine a set of glass tubes filled with lead shot and cotton wool, the sort from psycho-physical experiments in psychology laboratories. The sizes and weights may be made to vary independently. If we employ letters to represent weight (so that B is heavier than A, C is heavier than B, and so on) and numbers to represent size (so that 2 is larger than 1, 3 is larger than 2, etc.) we may represent a set of these tubes as follows:

Increasing size
→

A_1	A_2	A_3	A_4
B_1	B_2	B_3	B_4
C_1	C_2	C_3	C_4
D_1	D_2	D_3	D_4

Increasing weight ↓

All tubes in one row are of the same weight, and all tubes in one column are of the same size. The weight differences between rows need not be equal; all that need be established is that $D > C > B > A$. Similarly, the size differences between columns need not be equal: the series $4 > 3 > 2 > 1$ in this example represents a rank order only. We can see that might be shown three pictures arranged as follows, and asked what picture should be put in the blank space.

Black dog	Brown dog
Black cat	?

A_3 is larger but lighter than D_2, A_2 is lighter than D_2 but of the same size, and so on. Many such relationships may be generated by this one–one multiplication of size and weight relations.

It is possible, of course, to apply this grouping to cases where the relationships are not independent, for example the case in which a liquid is poured from a thin vessel into a wide one, so that height and width vary proportionately. The child solves conservation problems when he appreciates the complex relationship "higher than but narrower than". Examples of independent variation are to be found in the later series of the Raven's Progressive Matrices Test that we mentioned at the start of this chapter. Further evidence that a child possesses this grouping is displayed when he solves more advanced seriation problems than were mentioned for grouping V. With grouping VIII the child can arrange a number of dolls in order, then give each doll its appropriately sized walking stick and shopping bag.

We may summarize these groupings, according to Piaget's latest presentation as follows:

		Classes	Relations
Additives	{ asymmetrical	I	V
	symmetrical	II	VI
Multiplicatives	{ co-univocal	III	VII
	bi-univocal	IV	VIII

(For the sake of completeness we should mention that there is a ninth grouping, namely the grouping of equalities. A relationship of equality may be considered to exhibit the following properties:

Closure	$(A = B) + (B = C) = (A = C)$
Associativity	$(A = B) + (B = C) = (A = C)$ may be rewritten
	$(A = B) + (A = C) = (B = C)$, without altering the meaning.
General identity	$(A = A)$
Reversibility	If $(A = B)$ then $(B = A)$
Special identities	e.g. $(A = B) + (A = B) = (A = B)$.

The relationships among equalities are presupposed by all the major groupings listed, because if a child can maintain that, of three pieces of wood, the first is equal to the second and the second equal to the third (in whatever respect we choose), and yet deny that the first equals the third, he is not yet ready for operational thinking.)

The five properties of grouping may be traced in every one of these groupings, but, as we have indicated, we shall not detail them here. There is, nevertheless, one important point that we must note. Let us consider reversibility as applied to grouping **V** and ask "How does one reverse the relation 'A is greater than B'?" If we remember that to reverse a simple addition (as in grouping

I) we simply subtract, thus $A + A' = B$, so $B - A' = A$, we see that we end at our starting point. However, if we try to apply this operation to an ordered class difference, the result is not our starting point because (A is greater than B) $-$ (B is greater than A) means, if it means anything at all, that $A = B$. An alternative way of reversing this relationship is to re-express it, thus "A is greater than B" $=$ "B is smaller than A". Piaget calls this form of reversibility *reciprocity*. Reversibility, therefore, takes two forms (reciprocity and inversion); *inversion is the form of reversibility proper to classes, whereas reciprocity is proper to relations.*

The Language of Symbolic Logic

The principles of symbolism are fundamentally very simple, and to illustrate them we cannot do better than quote the passage from Jerome K. Jerome that Morris Kline quotes for the same purpose.

> When a twelfth-century youth fell in love he did not take three paces backward, gaze into her eyes, and tell her she was too beautiful to live. He said he would step outside and see about it. And if, when he got out, he met a man and broke his head—the other man's head, I mean—then that proved that his—the first fellow's—girl was a pretty girl. But if the other fellow broke his head—not his own, you know, but the other fellow's—the other fellow to the second fellow, that is, because of course the other fellow would only be the other fellow to him, not the first fellow who—well, if he broke his head, then his girl—not the other fellow's, but the fellow who was the—Look here, if A broke B's head, then A's girl was a pretty girl; but if B broke A's head, then A's girl wasn't a pretty girl, but B's girl was.

Kline observes that "while clever symbolism enables the mind to carry complicated ideas with ease, it also makes it harder for the layman to follow or understand a mathematical discussion". We are not going to discuss mathematics here, but we hope to make clear the ways in which logicians express the relationships between propositions. The use of symbols has the unfortunate consequence that many readers assume, at the very sight of them, that the ensuing discussion is going to be both mathematical and difficult. We have promised that our discussion will not be mathematical, and we shall try not to make it difficult.

Logicians commonly use the letters p and q to stand for propositions. (A proposition is the meaning of a statement as distinct from the form of words in which it is expressed. For instance, "a dog has four legs", "un chien a quatre jambes", "ein Hund hat vier Beine" all say the same thing in different ways: it does not matter which of these three expressions we choose, we are expressing the same proposition.) From the passage that we have quoted we may select three propositions for purposes of illustration:

(1) *A* broke *B*'s head.
(2) *A*'s girl was a pretty girl.
(3) *A*'s girl was not a pretty girl.
Let us add another proposition.
(4) *A* did not break *B*'s head.

Let us call (1) p and (2) q. We may call (3) $\bar{q}$ and (4) $\bar{p}$. (The symbol⁻ stands for *negation*.)

We now have four propositions, represented by p, $\bar{p}$, q, and $\bar{q}$ respectively, and we may express various degrees of relationship between them. For example, the sign $\supset$ is short for "if—then", so $p \supset q$ means "if p then q".* Translating this into English, "If *A* broke *B*'s head, then *A*'s girl was a pretty girl". The sign $\supset$ indicates the relationship known as *implication*.

In addition to the sign for implication, there are three other signs that we must learn. Two of them (we shall give the third later) are:

$\lor$ which stands for disjunction: $p \lor q$ means "either p or q or both".

* More fully "if p is true, then q is true".

which stands for conjunction: $p.q$ means "both p and q".

Now let us see how we can express various conclusions based on our understanding of relationships. Consider $p \supset q$, which, we remember, means "if p then q". This relationship could hold in the following cases.

(i) Both p and q are true $(p.q)$.
(ii) p is false but q is true $(\bar{p}.\bar{q})$.
(iii) Both p and q are false $(\bar{p}.\bar{q})$.

The one condition with which $p \supset q$ is incompatible is for p to be true but q false $(p.\bar{q})$. Now we may introduce the third symbol mentioned in the previous paragraph:

/ stands for *incompatibility*: $p \supset q / p.\bar{q}$ means "the relationship 'if p then q' is incompatible with the simultaneous truth of p and the falsity of q".

This example illustrates the brevity that is possible when we employ symbols. A more striking example is provided if we summarize all that we have written so far, both in English and in symbols. " 'If p then q' is compatible with either the truth of p and q; or the falsity of p and the truth of q; or the falsity of both p and q. It is incompatible with the simultaneous truth of p and the falsity of q."

$$p \supset q = (p.q) \vee (\bar{p}.q) \vee (\bar{p}.\bar{q}) \text{ but } p \supset q / p.\bar{q}.$$

Now let us work out the conditions under which $p \vee q$ is true. "Either p or q or both" is compatible with the truth of both p and q; the truth of p and the falsity of q; the falsity of p and the truth of q. It is incompatible with the falsity of both p and q. In terms of symbols:

$$p \vee q = (p.q) \vee (p.\bar{q}) \vee (\bar{p}.q) \text{ but } p \vee q / \bar{p}.\bar{q}.$$

In terms of Piaget's logic, $p.\bar{q}$ is the inverse of $p \supset q$: and $\bar{p}.\bar{q}$ is the inverse of $p \vee q$.

Inversion, as we know, is one form of reversibility in Piaget's system, the other being reciprocity (see p. 67). Reciprocity, we remember, refers to a re-expression of a proposition that reverses the direction of relationship. Our example was that the reciprocal of $A > B$ is $B < A$. *In logical terms, the reciprocal of $p \supset q$ is $q \supset p$. The reciprocal of $p \lor q$ is $\bar{p} \lor \bar{q}$.* (The reciprocal of $p = q$ is $\bar{p} = \bar{q}$.)

We have illustrated the use of symbols to describe the logic of relationships, but, to conclude this section, we must note that symbols may also be used to express the logic of classes. For instance, we know that if a creature is a dog it is a mammal, because the class of dogs is included in the class of mammals: we may formally represent the proposition "if a creature is a dog, then it is a mammal" by the symbols $p \supset q$.

Logic and Psychology

The reader may by now be wondering what the previous section has to do with psychology. We have seen that we *can* use symbols to describe the logic of classes and relations, but why *should* we? What special contribution does logic make to psychology?

Piaget maintains that the problem of the relationship between logic and psychology is of practical, as well as theoretical, interest. To take the theoretical question first, it would be interesting to know if logical structures and thinking are two sides of the same coin, so that, to put the problem in rather archaic language, the "laws of logic" are the "laws of thinking". This question has exercised philosophers for centuries, and is still far from being solved. The practical interest is in the potential contributions of logic to the advancement of psychological research. Piaget believes that we may think of logical structures as models for mental operations. If we keep these structures in mind as we investigate specimens of thinking, we have an ideal tool for the analysis of thinking (see Piaget, 1953a).

This notion is not as unfamiliar as it may seem. When one whistles a tune, the tune normally conforms (more or less) to the principles of tonal music, just as when three or four people spontaneously harmonize a song they do so according to the principles of Western harmony. Singers may sing well or badly, but they need not understand musical theory in order to succeed. Nevertheless, the principles of tonality and harmony may be considered to model their thinking, and may be taken as the criteria of successful music making. In much the same way, algebraic logic may be regarded as a model of thinking, and this model will assist the psychologist's analysis of children's and adolescents' thinking.

The Limitations of the Concrete Operations Phase

In the phase of concrete operations, the child is often able to solve problems with which he is faced, but his solutions are characteristically in terms of direct experience. For instance, acids turn blue litmus paper red, but this characteristic does not define acids. It is therefore not a contradiction in terms to speak of an acid that does not have this property, but if we asked a 9-year-old with some experience of general science "What would you say if you came across an acid that did not turn blue litmus paper red?" he would not understand the question. A typical reply to this question, from a child in the concrete operations phase, would be: "Then it would not be an acid." An adolescent, by contrast, would probably answer: "Then we should have to modify our proposition that all acids turn blue litmus paper red."

Let us examine the difference between these replies in logical terms. The child is arguing $p \supset q$ (if X is an acid then it turns blue litmus paper red); faced with an example of $\bar{q}$ (X does not turn blue litmus paper red), he replies $\bar{p}$ (X is not an acid). We have as before two propositions, each of which can have two values (true or false).* There are four conceivable combinations of these propositions: $p.q$, $p.\bar{q}$, $\bar{p}.q$, $\bar{p}.\bar{q}$.

* Hence the description of this logic as "two-valued propositional logic".

We may represent the relationships between them in the form of a table, as follows:

	p	$\dot{p}$
q	$+$	
$\bar{q}$		

indicates that $p.q$ is true. Both the child and the adolescent recognize that $p.q$ is true in the case of acids and blue litmus paper; but the difference is that the adolescent can appreciate the conceptual possibility of the other combinations, whereas the child cannot.

It is important to note that we cannot be sure that the child's argument about acid and litmus paper does illustrate the relationship of implication $p \supset q$. The child could well be arguing "acids are included in the class of things that turn blue litmus paper red". Diagrammatically this may be represented as follows:

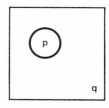

where p stands for "acids" and q for "the class of things that turn blue litmus paper red". The point is that from just one example we cannot be sure which model is appropriate to a child's thinking; we need to examine every aspect of the child's thinking before we can be sure. However, as we have seen, both class inclusion and propositional relationships are models of concrete operational thinking.

The difference between the concrete operations phase and the formal operations phase is fundamentally this: *The child in the concrete operations phase is concerned with the actual; the adolescent in the formal operations phase is concerned with the possible and its relation to the actual.* It follows that formal operational thinking is charact-erized by an appreciation of the totality of relationships between propositions, and for this reason the formal operations phase is often called the phase of propositional operations.

Formal operational thinking is further distinguished from con-crete operational thinking in being more coherent. For instance, the two forms of reversibility (inversion and reciprocity) become integrated into a single system, so there are no longer two logics (of classes and relations respectively) but one logic, which, as we shall see, has the characteristics of both a group and a lattice.

The Phase of Formal Operations

We have said that formal operational thinking has the charact-eristics of both a group and a lattice (which means, of course, that it has the nature of a grouping—Piaget calls it a "higher-order grouping"). Let us start by illustrating the group character-istic.

Now we have seen how to indicate negation, inversion, and reciprocity. To make our account complete we must explain a fourth term, namely *correlation*. We obtain the correlate of an expression by substituting . whenever $\vee$ occurs, and vice versa. In case this seems a little too mysterious to be acceptable, let us think if the conditions under which $p.q$ may be true. What $p.q$ means is that "p and q are simultaneously true". Clearly this is incompatible with the falsity of either p or q, but it *is* compatible with the falsity of both, i.e. $p.q = \bar{p}.\bar{q}$. But $\bar{p}.\bar{q}$ is incompatible with $p \vee q$, so the only condition with which $p.q$ is *compatible* is the condition with which $p \vee q$ is *incompatible*. Piaget calls $p \vee q$ the correlate of $p.q$ (and, of course, $p.q$ is the correlate of $p \vee q$).

Let us now try to express some relations in tabular form, using the following abbreviations:

$$I = \text{identity} \qquad C = \text{correlation}$$
$$R = \text{reciprocity} \qquad N = \text{inversion}$$

We may start from $p \vee q$.

The reciprocal of $p \vee q$ is $\bar{p} \vee \bar{q}$ (and vice versa), so we may write:

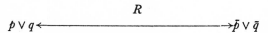

We have defined the correlate of $p \vee q$ as $p.q$, and the correlate of $\bar{p} \vee \bar{q}$ must (from our definitions) be $\bar{p}.\bar{q}$, so we may extend our table as follows:

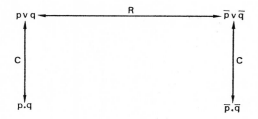

Now if the reciprocal of $p \vee q$ is $\bar{p} \vee \bar{q}$, then the reciprocal of $p.q$ must be $\bar{p}.\bar{q}$, so we may draw a fourth line:

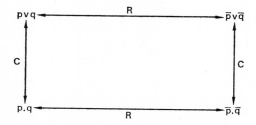

We have already seen (p. 69) that $\bar{p}.\bar{q}$ is the inverse of $p \vee q$. Similarly, the inverse of $p.q$, is $\bar{p} \vee \bar{q}$, so we may complete our table as follows:

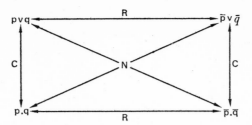

Now let us look at some of the relationships within this table. If we start from $p \vee q$, obtain its reciprocal, and then the correlate of the reciprocal, we arrive at the inverse of $p \vee q$. In terms of abbreviations, $RC = N$. Alternatively, of course, $CR = N$, $NC = R$, $NR = C$. To take this further, if we start from any corner of the table, take the reciprocal, then the inverse of this reciprocal, then the correlate of this inverse, we return to our starting point, so $RNC = I$. Similarly, $NCR = I$, $CRN = I$, $CNR = I$.

It is possible to construct similar tables of transformations starting from other relationships, e.g. $p \supset q$.

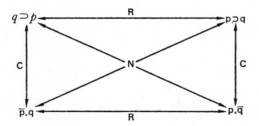

The student may suspect that an example of symbolic sleight of hand has taken place here because it is not immediately clear that $\bar{p}.\bar{q}$ is the correlate of $q \supset p$, or that the correlate of $p.\bar{q}$ is $p \supset q$. In fact the truth of these transformations is easily demonstrated (the student may care to attempt the demonstration himself before reading the next paragraph).

We obtain a correlate by substituting $\vee$ for . in an expression of relationship. If we substitute ∨ for . in $\bar{p}.q$ we obtain $\bar{p} \vee q$. Now from what we have seen above, $\bar{p} \vee q = (\bar{p}.q) \vee (p.q) \vee (\bar{p}.\bar{q})$ but $\bar{p} \vee q / p.\bar{q}$. Now the only relationship with which $p \supset q$ is incompatible is also $p.\bar{q}$. We may therefore write $p \supset q$ for $\bar{p} \vee q$, the correlate of $\bar{p}.q$. Similarly, we may write $q \supset p$ for $p \vee \bar{q}$, the correlate of $p.\bar{q}$.

The four transformations (*INRC*) form a group because they have the principles of closure (no matter how we combine them, we obtain one of the four); associativity (the order in which we combine the transformations does not affect the outcome, thus $CRN = CNR$, $NCR = RCN = CRN = I$); general identity (this is the identity element itself, e.g. $(CRI = CR)$; and reversibility (it is always possible to reverse one's steps by taking steps in the opposite direction, i.e. every arrow has a head at each end). This group is often called the "four group".

We now turn to the lattice characteristic of formal operational thinking.

We have already introduced the notion of a truth table. Let us now consider the truth tables for the four propositional combinations $p.q$, $p.\bar{q}$, $\bar{p}.q$, and $\bar{p}.\bar{q}$. They are as follows:

(i) $p.q$

(ii) $p.\bar{q}$

(iii) $\bar{p}.q$

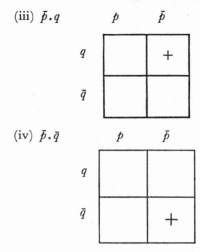

(iv) $\bar{p}.\bar{q}$

To what would an empty table correspond? A table in which every cell was empty must mean that none of the combinations (i) to (iv) listed above was true. We may describe this as the *null condition*.

It is possible to combine the combinations in various ways. For instance $(p.q) \lor (p.\bar{q})$ means "either p is true and q is true, or p is true and q is false". In other words, the truth of p is independent of the truth of q. We may represent this in tabular form by superimposing tables (i) and (ii). Thus we obtain:

(i) + (ii)

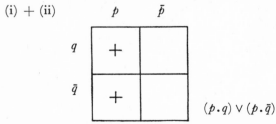

$(p.q) \lor (p.\bar{q})$

We may represent other combinations similarly, but for ease of setting out we shall not write the values of p and q around the tables. The combinations are as follows:

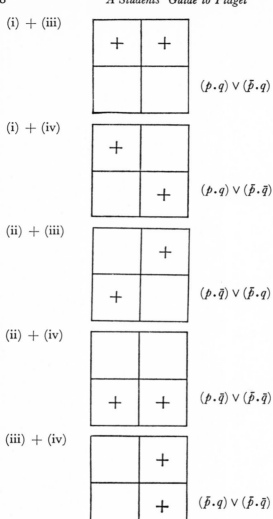

(i) + (iii)

$(p.q) \vee (\bar{p}.q)$

(i) + (iv)

$(p.q) \vee (\bar{p}.\bar{q})$

(ii) + (iii)

$(p.\bar{q}) \vee (\bar{p}.q)$

(ii) + (iv)

$(p.\bar{q}) \vee (\bar{p}.\bar{q})$

(iii) + (iv)

$(\bar{p}.q) \vee (\bar{p}.\bar{q})$

The effect of combining any one of these combinations with the null combination is, of course, to leave the table unchanged.

We may combine the basic combinations in more ways than those shown. For instance, we may have:

$$(\text{i}) + (\text{ii}) + (\text{iii}) = (p.q) \lor (p.\bar{q}) \lor (\bar{p}.q)$$

Superimposing the corresponding tables yields the following:

+	+
+	

Similarly

(i) + (iii) + (iv)

+	+
	+

$(p.q) \lor (\bar{p}.q) \lor (\bar{p}.\bar{q})$

(i) + (ii) + (iv)

+	
+	+

$(p.q) \lor (p.\bar{q}) \lor (\bar{p}.\bar{q})$

(ii) + (iii) + (iv)

	+
+	+

$(p.\bar{q}) \lor (\bar{p}.q) \lor (\bar{p}.\bar{q})$

(i) + (ii) + (iii) +
   (iv)

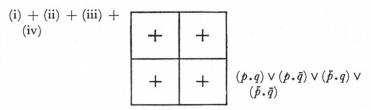

$(p \cdot q) \vee (p \cdot \bar{q}) \vee (\bar{p} \cdot q) \vee (\bar{p} \cdot \bar{q})$

To complete this account, we may give the symbolic equivalent of the empty table.

It is: $\overline{(p \cdot q) \vee (p \cdot \bar{q}) \vee (\bar{p} \cdot q) \vee \bar{p} \cdot \bar{q})}$

Table 4.1 lists and numbers the combinations that we have looked at so far.

TABLE 4.1. THE SIXTEEN BINARY OPERATIONS DERIVED FROM COMBINATIONS OF
$p \cdot q, \, p \cdot \bar{q}, \, \bar{p} \cdot q, \, \bar{p} \cdot \bar{q}.$

1. 0   (The null combination)
2. (i)
3. (ii)
4. (iii)
5. (iv)
6. (i) + (ii)
7. (i) + (iii)
8. (i) + (iv)
9. (ii) + (iii)
10. (ii) + (iv)
11. (iii) + (iv)
12. (i) + (ii) + (iii)
13. (i) + (iii) + (iv)
14. (i) + (ii) + (iv)
15. (ii) + (iii) + (iv)
16. (i) + (ii) + (iii) + (iv)

These sixteen combinations are called *binary operations* (because they are derived by combining the four unitary values p, $\bar{p}$, q, and $\bar{q}$).

In Fig. 4.1 we have set out the relationships between the sixteen truth tables corresponding to the binary operations. Two examples will explain how this figure is to be interpreted. Truth table 12 is made up of tables 6, 7, and 9. If we refer to Table 4.1

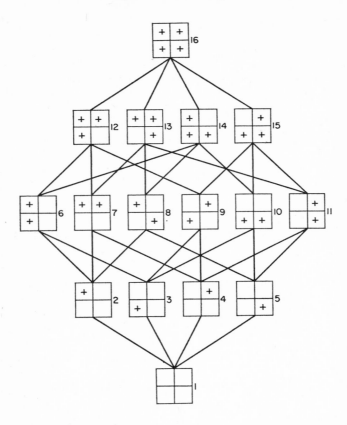

FIG. 4.1. Relations between the truth tables for sixteen binary operations
(modified from Baldwin, 1967).

we find that operation 12 is compounded of operations (i), (ii),
and (iii). Table 4.1 also tells us that operation 6 is made up of
operations (i) and (ii), 7 is made up of (i) + (iii), 9 is made up of
(ii) and (iii). If we return to Fig. 4.1 we find that table 6 is com-
posed of tables 2 (representing operation (i)) and 3 (representing
operation (ii)).

For our second example we see that tables 6 and 7 are connected to table 2. Truth table 2 in fact, shows what tables 6 and 7 have in common. If we refer to Table 4.1 we find that operation 6 equals operation (i) plus (ii), whilst operation 7 equals operations (i) + (iii). What 6 and 7 have in common, therefore, is operation (i) (i.e. $p.q$), which in tabular form is:

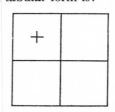

as shown in Fig. 4.1.

These examples should remind us of an earlier example. If for operation 6 we write "dogs", writing "poodles" for operation 2 and "dogs other than poodles" for operation 3, we see immediately that the relations between the sixteen binary operations have lattice properties. In fact, Fig. 4.1 is a complete lattice, because every two elements of the table have both a greatest lower bound and a least upper bound. There is no need for further examples as inspection of the figure will confirm its lattice structure.

Let us see how we may simplify our expressions of the binary operations. Consider operation 12, which equals $(p.q) \vee (p.\bar{q}).(\bar{p}.q)$. What this tells us is that, when p is true, q may be either true or false, but that when p is false, then q is true. In other words $\bar{p} \supset q$. To show this more clearly, let us write out the conditions with which $\bar{p} \supset q$ is compatible or incompatible (as we did $p \supset q$ on p. 69). The conditions are as follows:

$$\bar{p} \supset q = (p.q) \vee (p.\bar{q})(\vee \bar{p}.q)$$
$$\text{but } \bar{p} \supset q / \bar{p} \ . \ \bar{q}$$

Truth table 12 shows that the cells corresponding to $p.q$, $p.\bar{q}$, and $\bar{p}.q$ are occupied, but that the cell corresponding to $\bar{p}.\bar{q}$ is empty. Therefore for operation 12 we may write $\bar{p} \supset q$.

Similarly operation 13 is equivalent to $p \supset q$, operation 14 to $\bar{p} \supset \bar{q}$, and operation 15 to $p \supset \bar{q}$. (The student is advised to confirm these equivalences for himself.)

Let us look at operations 6–11. Operation 6 asserts $(p.q) \vee (p.\bar{q})$, in other words, that p is true whether or not q is true, or, more simply, that p is true. Similarly, operation 7 asserts that q is true. Operation 8 states that when p is true q is true, and that when p is false q is false, or simply that $p = q$. Operation 9 asserts, by contrast, that when p is true q is false, and when p is false q is true, or p/q (p and q are incompatible). It will by now be obvious that operation 10 is equivalent to asserting that q is false ($\bar{q}$), and operation 11 is equivalent to $\bar{p}$.

We already know that operations 2–5 are $p.q$, $\bar{p}.q$, $p.\bar{q}$, and $\bar{p}.\bar{q}$ respectively, so we may rewrite our table of relationships as in Fig. 4.2.

16

p and q are independent

	12 $p \supset q$	13 $p \supset q$	14 $p \supset \bar{q}$	15 $p \supset \bar{q}$	
6 p	7 q	8 $p = q$	9 p/q	10 $\bar{q}$	11 p
	2 $p \cdot q$	3 $\bar{p} \cdot q$	4 $p \cdot \bar{q}$	5 $\bar{p} \cdot \bar{q}$	

1

null

FIG. 4.2. The sixteen binary operations expressed as propositional relations.

It is easy to see from Fig. 4.2 how more complex relationships might be expressed: for instance, $\bar{p}.(\bar{p} \supset q)$ means "p is false, and the falsity of p implies the truth of q". By combining together the sixteen binary operations, we should obtain 256 (i.e. 16×16) *tertiary* operations. We could even obtain 65,536 *quaternary* operations by combining together the 256 tertiary operations. Although adolescent and adult thinking makes use of these higher order combinations, we do not propose to illustrate them here, as the principle of combinational operations should be clear from our discussion of binary operations.

Attainments of the Formal Operations Phase

The beginning of the formal operations phase marks the transition from childhood to adolescence. The adolescent has an expanded time scale, and can think about the future. Furthermore, because of his newly discovered power of thinking symbolically and constructing concepts not directly related to actual situations, he is able to manipulate ideas not directly related to the real world. This has the paradoxical effect of making him both more and less effective socially: more because he can understand even better than before the relativity of view points; less, because he is imbued with a belief in the omnipotence of thinking. With respect to the second point, we see here a recrudescence of the egocentricity of the earlier years. Because he is able to conceive of a situation, the adolescent is apt to believe that things can be as he conceives them; only with increasing maturity does he come to think realistically, that is to distinguish between what is conceptually possible and what is attainable in fact. This is possible only through experience in the real world, which includes encounters with others, with whom he may share ideas.

Full maturity in the sense that we have been discussing is probably seldom achieved before early adulthood, but our major concern in these chapters is with the development of patterns of reasoning, which, for Piaget, is complete at between 14 and 15 years. Therefore we shall conclude this chapter by describing two reasoning problems that, typically, are solved successfully only in the phase of formal operations (Inhelder and Piaget, 1958).

The first example we shall choose is from an experiment in which children and adolescents were asked to mix four unnamed colourless chemical solutions together in order to produce a coloured liquid in combination with a fifth solution. The child is given four identical flasks, containing respectively (1) dilute sulphuric acid, (2) water, (3) oxygenated water, (4) sodium thiosulphate (all these are colourless), and a smaller flask containing potassium iodide (called flask g). Before the experiment the experimenter fills two beakers, (i) containing dilute sulphuric acid and oxygenated water, (ii) containing water (both (i) and (ii) are, of course, colourless). In the subject's presence he adds several drops of potassium iodide from the smaller flask to beakers (i) and (ii). The liquid in beaker (i) turns yellow, whilst that in beaker (ii) does not.

The reason for the difference is that the oxygenated water oxidizes potassium iodide in an acid medium. For the experiment to be meaningful the subject must not, of course, know the chemical action. He must mix the contents of flasks 1–4 in various ways in order to achieve the desired effect with the potassium iodide.

To achieve success, the subject must mix 1 with 3 but not add 4, because sodium thiosulphate reacts with the potassium iodide, leaving the result colourless. (In effect, adding 4 to $1 + 3 + 2$ reverses the action, so the act of adding 4 is effectively to achieve reciprocity.)

By means of this experiment (and similar experiments, involving the use of burettes of acids and alkalis, and chemical indicators) we can trace the growth of the combination system from the earliest stages, where it is limited to multiplying each of the "factors" 1 to 4 by g; through an unsystematic attempt at combination, involving trial and error; to the systematic combination of the formal operations stage.

We can see that the system of propositional relations and their combination can be used as a model for the successful solution of this task because if we let p stand for "colour" and q for "contents of flask 2" (i.e. water) we may describe the effect of adding 2 to $1 + 3 + g$ as follows: $(p.q) \vee (p.\bar{q}) \vee (\bar{p}.q) \vee (\bar{p}.\bar{q})$. In other words, flask 2 has no effect. If, on the other hand, we let q stand for "contents of flask 4" (sodium thiosulphate), we have $(p.\bar{q}) \vee (\bar{p}.q)$, that is to say that colour is present when the contents of flask 4 are absent; and colour is absent when the contents of flask 4 are present, so colour and flask 4 are incompatible (p/q). As for the combination aspect of the operation, we see this in the formal operations stage because the adolescent no longer looks for the colour in one or other of the elements but in their being combined in certain ways. In other words, the child's reasoning is not $p \supset x$ (if the colour appears, then substance must be present) but $p \supset (x.y.z)$ (if the colour appears, three things must be combined).

Piaget regards the understanding of combination, as revealed by this experiment, as essentially identical with the system of binary operations. It is for this reason that the ability to solve problems involving combinations of substances appears at the same time as the understanding of the combination of propositions. As Piaget puts it, "from the subject's point of view the only purpose of the combinational operations applied to the experimental data is to make it possible for him to establish—logical connections"(Inhelder and Piaget, 1958). To put it another way, the adolescent's mental abilities form an equilibrium in which problem solving and the structure of thinking are revealed in his relationships with the world around him. Because he employs his structured thinking in his adaptation to the world, we may say that he is employing *formal operational schemata.*

The formal operational schema just described involved the lattice structure. To conclude this chapter, we shall describe a formal operation schema involving the groups structure. The child is presented with a simple balance and some weights: for younger children the weights may take the form of dolls, and the balance-pans the form of baby carriages, but for adolescents the weights are conventional in type, and of 5, 10, 15, and 20 units respectively. The weights may be inserted in holes spaced regularly along the arms of the balance.

In this situation, the downward pull exerted on the balance arm is a product of the weight and its distance from the fulcrum (this product is called the "moment of inertia"). Equal weights at different distances will make the balance tilt, whilst unequal weights at suitable distances will put the balance in equilibrium.

By arranging different combinations of weights and distances, and asking children and adolescents to explain the outcome, the experimenter can investigate the growth of the understanding of the principles involved.

Full understanding comes only with the stage of formal operations, because the principles involved can only be fully described by the four group (*INRC*) described on p. 76. If we increase the weight on one arm, we can restore equilibrium by increasing the weight on the other arm by increasing its distance from the fulcrum or both. Let us represent an increase in weight by p and increase in distance by q; then $\bar{p}$ symbolizes a decrease in weight, whilst $\bar{q}$ symbolizes a decrease in distance. We may call the restoration of equilibrium by increasing weight and distance the identity operation I. Then $I = p.q$.

If the balance is put out of equilibrium, we could invert the action by either decreasing the weight $\bar{p}$ or decreasing the distance $\bar{q}$. Thus $N = (\bar{p} \vee \bar{q})$. We could restore the equilibrium by increasing weight and distance on the other balance arm, an action that we may symbolize as $p'.q'$. This is, of course, a reversal by reciprocity. But increasing weight and distance on arm A is equivalent to decreasing weight and distance on arm B, so $p'.q' = \bar{p}.\bar{q}$. So $R = \bar{p}.\bar{q}$.

Another way of altering the effect of $p.q$ is by *decreasing* weight or distance on arm A, $\bar{p}' \vee \bar{q}'$. But the effect of decreasing these weights or distances on arm A is the same as increasing them on arm B, so $\bar{p}' \vee \bar{q}' = p \vee q$.

To summarize, we have:

$$I = p.q \qquad R = \bar{p}.\bar{q}$$
$$N = \bar{p} \vee \bar{q} \qquad C = p \vee q$$

This reasoning may seem very abstruse, but the essential point is, as always, that these transformations of propositional relations provide the most suitable model for describing the adolescent's problem-solving processes. The adolescent is not aware of these transformations, but the types of explanation that he offers of the problems that he is set show that his thinking does conform to this model.

It is fair to observe, as a closing note, that Piaget's use of logic has not found universal favour among logicians. However, we must defer critical considerations to later chapters.

CHAPTER 5

A Brief Summary of Developmental Periods in Piaget's Psychology

IN THIS chapter we shall summarize the course of human development as presented in Chapters 2, 3, and 4. The scheme that we have adopted for the purpose of exposition can in no sense be regarded as definitive, since Piaget's commentators, not to mention Piaget himself, are not always consistent in their presentation. In particular the terms "phase", "stage", and "period" are often used interchangeably. In the scheme adopted for this book, *phase* describes a major division in the course of development, *stage* refers to a subdivision of a phase, whilst *period* is employed as a generic term, comprising both phase and stage.

The ages given for the various developmental periods are those that one customarily finds in accounts of Piaget's work. However, as we saw in Chapter 2 (p. 27) the ages are only approximations. They are, generally speaking, the rough limits of the ages of the children whom Piaget studied, and who had attained these periods. The fact that many children may reach these periods at very different ages is no criticism of Piaget, for even in Piaget's protocols we often find considerable overlaps of ages and developmental periods. The important consideration is not the timing of the periods, but their sequence.

I. *Sensorimotor Phase*   0–2 years

The phase is characterized by rhythmical repetition of circular reactions, and comprises a progress from autism to egocentricity.

1. Stage of random and reflex action	0–1 month
2. Stage of primary circular reactions and the first schemata	1–4 months
3. Stage of secondary circular reactions and "procédés pour faire continuer un spectacle interessant"	4–8 months
4. Stage of co-ordination of secondary schemata and their application to new situations	8–12 months
5. Stage of tertiary circular reactions, with the discovery, through active experimentation, of new means to gain desired ends	12–18 months
6. Stage of invention of new means by mental combinations rather than actions, that is to say the appearance of elementary memory and planning	18–24 months

II. *Pre-operational Phase*   2–7 years

This phase comprises the progress from sensorimotor organization to the beginnings of internalization of actions to form operations. Whereas at first the child centres his attention on only one aspect of a situation, thus failing to grasp the invariance of physical properties in materials undergoing transformations, he later regulates his thinking by paying attention to aspects undergoing reciprocal changes. This decentring of attention permits development of the notion of permanence of physical properties, because it facilitates mental manipulation of actions, including reversing an action and returning to the starting point.

1. Preconceptual stage	2–4 years

   The young child is unable to perform abstractions and generalizations and thus cannot form concepts or handle classes. Nevertheless, he uses some words in a "semi-generic" way to indicate "another of the same type", and is said to have "pre-concepts".

2. Intuitive stage.   4–7 years
   The child solves simple problems involving
   number, time, space, etc., and shows by
   his behaviour that he understands, in general terms, the elements of co-operative play
   long before he is able to explain how he
   knows these things. He appears to have an
   intuitive grasp of physical and social properties and relationships. The egocentrism
   of the previous stage gives way, during the
   present stage, to socially directed thought
   and action.

III. *Phase of Concrete Operations*   7–11½ years

This phase is marked by an equilibrium between accommodation and assimilation, which is revealed by a more exten-
sive use of reversibility in thinking. Reversibility characterizes
this phase as rhythm characterizes Phase I and regulation Phase
II, but the two forms of reversibility (inversion and reciprocity—
proper to classes and relations respectively) are not integrated
into a whole. The child can classify in terms of semi-lattices,
Models for his thinking may be found in mathematical groups.
and in groupings, which have features of both groups and lattices.
However, the application of these is fragmentary, and they are
applied to different subject-matters at different ages. Social
competence is increased by the development of understanding
of the relativity of viewpoints.

IV. *Phase of Formal Operations*   11½ years onwards

The beginning of the formal operations phase coincides
approximately with the onset of adolescence. The adolescent's
thinking is more coherent in structure than the child's, and has
features of both a group and a complete lattice. The two forms of
reversibility are integrated into a group of four transformations
(identity I, inversion N, reciprocity R, and correlation C). The
lattice structure is given by the interrelationships of the sixteen

binary operations of two-valued propositional logic. The adolescent's thinking is concerned much more with propositions than with physical situations, which means that he is able to deal mentally with the conceivably possible rather than just the actual, and to understand the relationship of the possible to the actual. This relationship appears first in the physical field where, by the age of about 15 years, he is able to formulate explanations of phenomena (such as the results of chemical combinations and moments of inertia) which he could not explain without the group and lattice properties of formal operational thinking. The ways in which he integrates his new intellectual capacities for explanatory purposes are called formal operational schemata. In the social field he is at first less able to distinguish the possible from the actual, and for some years behaves as if he believes in the omnipotence of thought. Thus we see a form of egocentricity, analogous to that of earlier years, which, through continued social interchange, gives way to an understanding of social realities.

To relate this summary to the preceding chapters we shall remind the reader that Phases I and II have been discussed in Chapter 3, Phases III and IV in Chapter 4.

III

EPISTEMOLOGY AND PSYCHOLOGY

CHAPTER 6

Piaget's Solutions to the Problems of Mathematical Epistemology*

THE problems of mathematical epistemology are not the same for a philosopher and a psychologist: the logical problem is to determine the conditions under which a mathematical demonstration can be accepted as valid, whereas the psychological problem is to investigate the mental mechanisms whereby the demonstration actually develops in the mathematician's mind. However, these problems are not readily separated in practice, and we have seen (in Chapter 1 of this book) that philosophers have often made use of psychological speculations in considering how the sciences of pure logic and mathematics are possible; conversely Piaget believes that his genetic psychology will shed light on such problems as the validity of mathematical constructions.

Piaget's developmental studies have forced him to the conclusion that the refinement of deductive methods does not represent a qualitatively new departure from the natural process of growth; instead we must regard it as a natural development of intelligence. Just as each phase of development from birth to maturity "transcends" earlier developmental levels whilst being a continuation of them, so advanced mathematical thinking transcends previous thinking whilst continuing it. Now we have seen that thinking for Piaget represents an internalizing of the subject's actions, so Piaget is arguing that the intrinsic features of logic originate in human actions. In the light of this viewpoint let us first see how Piaget deals with the crucial question of the

---

* This chapter is based on Piaget's section of Beth and Piaget (1966).

"self-evident" nature of mathematical truths, (see pp. 16–17 of this book).

If we tell an adult that *A* is longer than *B*, and *B* is longer than *C*, he will tell us that it is self-evident that *A* is longer than *C*. A 5-year-old child will not regard this as self-evident, and his failure to do so does not represent a failure to understand the question. We can demonstrate this by showing him two sticks, which we may call *A* and *B*, which differ in length, then removing the longer *A* and replacing it with a third stick *C*, which is shorter than *B*. The child will admit that *B* is longer than *C* and that *A* is longer than *B*, but may nevertheless deny that *A* is longer than *C*, unless *A* and *C* are placed side by side. A child of 7 years will have no such difficulty with the problem. Nevertheless, he will fail the problem if the physical variable is changed from one of length to one of weight; the "self-evidence" of transitivity with respect to weight comes a little later.

There is a problem to be explained here. A relationship that is self-evident to a child of one age in one type of situation may not be self-evident to the same child in another situation; and what is not self-evident to the child at one age will appear self-evident when he is older. Sometimes it may seem that the child's denial of the self-evident nature of a relationship is due to a lack of familiarity with particular situations, for some children attain this realization in the course of a Piagetian interrogation. However, these cases are only apparently exceptions to the general rule that a child is unable to grasp a relationship until his intelligence is sufficiently developed, and that different relationships require different levels of development for their understanding. Naturally both experience and development are required as development advances by means of the two-way process of assimilation and accommodation; but, in the absence of the appropriate development, experience will be ineffective.

What, then, is the nature of this development that makes understanding possible? Piaget explains it as the completion of the grouping with which a particular relationship is concerned (see Chapter 4). In the case of transitivity this grouping is seriation, which we know that the child has attained when he can systematically arrange in order a set of similar objects differing in one respect, for example a set of rods of different lengths. A 5-year-old will go about this unsystematically, taking the rods in twos and threes: if he succeeds at all it is by trial and error. The 7-year-old characteristically knows *in advance* how to set about the task, for he understands how to co-ordinate the relationships of "greater than" and "less than". Clearly, to a child who has attained the grouping of seriation, it will indeed be self-evident that, if *A* is greater than *B* and *C* is less than *B*, then *A* will be greater than *C*. (The reason why transitivity is appreciated for length before it is appreciated for weight is that groupings in the concrete operations phase are not integrated into a coherent whole—as we have seen (Chapter 4), this coherence is the prerequisite of the phase of formal operations.)

Just as self-evidence can be acquired, it may be lost, because it is "obvious" to a 3-year-old that, if one pours liquid from a tall glass into two or three shallow vessels, the quantity changes. Later on he will realize that this interpretation of the situation is false. This acquisition and loss of self-evidence in the child may be taken as a parallel to the progress of the history of ideas, and in particular to what Beth describes as "noetic integration" (see Chapter 1). Let us examine this parallel more closely.

We show a child two sticks equal in length, placed as follows: ——————————————— If we ask a 3-year-old "Are the sticks the same length?" he will agree that they are. Suppose that we now displace one of the sticks, so that they are lying as follows: ——————————————— The child will now deny that they are the same length. An older child, who has come to think in terms of reversibility (because his attention is no longer centred on just one end of the rods), will realize that the lengths remain the same. In effect he has come to assume (as self-evidently true) that length is not affected by movement. The same (tacit) assumption is found in Euclid's geometry as a strategy for solving problems involving equal triangles.

With the advent of relativity theory, Euclid's strategy had to be abandoned. What was self-evident when both time and space could be regarded as absolute was no longer self-evident in a relativistic universe. Here, then, is an example of the loss of self-evidence. What the young child and the mathematician have in common is that, when the nature of their self-evidence changes, it is because their previous thinking has become integrated into a wider framework that transcends the earlier thinking. This is true for physical science as well as mathematics, because even though the nature of self-evidence in the physical field is more vulnerable to contingent facts than in mathematics, these contingent facts are always integrated into systems of thinking (Conant, 1956). With regard to the development of mathematics, Piaget argues that we must think of this as akin to organic growth: although we cannot predict the direction that mathematics will take, we can show retrospectively that it has obeyed certain laws of direction. It is the particular contribution of genetic psychology to elucidate these laws.

Piaget's work, as we have seen, has led him to the conclusion that the development of intelligence is the result of a progressive equilibrium, revealed as adaptation to the environment (see Chapter 2). This equilibrium will begin by abstraction from actions and continue by reasoning about transformations (for instance, belief in the conservation of substance of a ball of dough squeezed in the hand, before the child understands weight and volume sufficiently clearly to be able to verify his belief). Therefore, although language and culture are important because by their means society can consolidate the various kinds of self-evidence found in logic and mathematics, they are not in themselves responsible for this self-evidence.

The problem of self-evidence is closely bound up with the question whether mathematical entities are invented or discovered, for if a new entity is a discovery we may suppose that it will be recognized by all mathematicians competent to judge, as being derived from self-evident truths, whereas this will not necessarily be so for an invention. If, however, the nature of self-evidence may change in the course of time, an entity may appear to be an invention to one age and a discovery to another. A study of the development of intellectual structures can shed light on this problem because when a new entity is accepted it is accepted into a framework of existing ideas which may be modified by its acceptance. It would seem legitimate to say that the framework had accommodated itself in order to assimilate the new entity.

This approach to the problem is, in Piaget's opinion, more satisfying than attempts to find an answer by way of introspection. We have seen (Chapter 1) that creative thinkers have stressed the importance of "unconscious work" in the creative process, and although Piaget feels that the distinction between conscious and unconscious work is relative rather than absolute, he recognizes that some mental processes are inaccessible to introspection. Furthermore, even when introspection is possible (as in reviewing the preparation for creative work and the subsequent verification of a new idea), it is subject to distortion from affective elements of the thinker's personality. Let us see, then, what a Piagetian approach can contribute to this problem.

The first thing that we must note is that many characteristics of organic structures may be described mathematically. The existence of organic structures is a necessary preliminary condition of thinking because thinking presupposes sensorimotor action, which is dependent upon neural and other organic structures. Physical structures are not preliminary conditions of thinking in the way that organic structures are because we can think without appealing to experience, the most notable example of this independence being pure mathematics. Organic structures presuppose physical structures, being derived from them, but the physical structures do not enter directly into the subject's thinking; they always enter through the activity of the organism. (As we have seen earlier in this chapter (p. 98), thinking derives from abstractions from the subject's action on physical objects, not from the objects themselves.)

If we may regard organic structures as psychological preliminaries of thought, we may also look on them as *epistemological* preliminaries. The reason why is that higher structures of thought are derived from lower structures by means of "reflective abstraction" (see Chapter 1, p. 17). Mathematical thinking derives from non-mathematical adult thinking by reflective abstraction, just as formal operational thinking derives from concrete operational thinking. Operations in their turn are derived by reflective abstraction from sensorimotor structures, which reflect neural structures. We may thus trace reflective abstraction back to organic structures, and see that it has no absolute starting point. Although these considerations may appear alien to the problem of mathematical invention, it is in their light that Piaget attempts to show that there is a third possibility between invention and discovery.

We may define an invention as the creation of a new and free combination of elements, even if the elements themselves were previously known, for instance a new demonstration of an already known theorem. To talk of a discovery, on the other hand, presupposes that something (be it entity or object) has previously existed, but that the subject has only just become aware of it. An establishment of a new theorem elucidating existing, but previously unrecognized, relationships between known entities is more akin to a discovery than to an invention. Even so, the distinction is a little arbitrary because pointing out previously unperceived relationships has some of the characteristics of an invention.

What, though, are we to say of $\sqrt{-1}$? At first this seemed like an invention, hence the term "imaginary" which was applied to it. In the light of later developments it seems rather to be a discovery. What has brought about its change of status?

The answer to such problems, Piaget says, is to be found in the nature of "reflective abstraction", by means of which mathematical entities are constructed.

We cannot describe reflective abstraction as a process of discovery, because the "reflected" structures are not identical with the structures from which they are derived; instead there is a reconstruction on a higher level of mental functioning, and this reconstruction in turn leads to a more general structure of thought. If this is how mathematical advance proceeds, then the new mathematical entity will both enrich the structure of mathematics and, because the new entity forms part of an enriched structure, be enriched in turn by the structure. Hence it must be more than a discovery.

At the same time, reflective abstraction cannot be pure invention because when we examine mathematics retrospectively we see that the entities that have been accepted have a character of necessity. It is important to note that we can only see this after the event because at any given time we cannot be aware of all the latent generalizations implicit in a mathematical structure. A new entity will be successful if its generalizations permit it to become part of a wider structure.

Piaget concludes that mathematical construction is neither invention nor discovery, but a process *sui generis*. If we are to say anything certain about this process, we must know all the logico-mathematical structures that are inherent in all developmental levels from the organic and morphogenetic structures up to the most advanced.

Piaget's concept of "reflective abstraction" is central to his view of intuition. We saw in Chapter 1 that mathematicians have often referred to intuition in their speculations on the origins of mathematics. Piaget points out that they have used the term in a number of ways without always specifying precisely what they mean by it; for instance, Helmholtz's attempt to derive the notion of ordinal number from our apprehension of successive states of consciousness employs a different notion of intuition from Poincaré's attempt to justify the primitive character of numerical iteration (see p. 52) by reference to an intuition that, however large a number, we may always add 1 to it.

One class of intuitions that has been proposed includes apprehension of self-evident truths such as "the whole is greater than its parts". The problem of the brown and wooden beads (p. 43) shows us that this is only relatively and not absolutely self-evident because it is not self-evident to the pre-operational child.

Piaget's account of self-evidence, discussed previously in this chapter, showed how the concept of reflective abstraction could explain the change in the self-evidential character of this proposition with age: the proposition is only seen to be self-evidently true when the intuition is part of the type of intellectual structure known as a grouping. We know that groupings arise by reflective abstraction. Similarly, we may employ the concept of reflective abstraction to rephrase the views of Helmholtz and Poincaré that were mentioned in the previous paragraph. Whereas Helmholtz believed that we derive our notion of number from states of consciousness, Piaget argues that we derive it from the actions that we perform on objects, and that these "objects" include states of consciousness. The "actions" that we perform on states of consciousness will include arranging them in order. Similarly, the notion of iteration is not derived from an intuition that we may always add 1 to a previous number, but arises by reflective abstraction from the child's earliest activities of arranging and ordering objects.

In short, with respect to intuition Piaget reiterates his view that there is an intimate connection between logico-mathematical entities and the subject's activities. As this is a controversial view, we must see how Piaget defends it.

We know that Piaget believes that the growth of intellectual structures comes about by the internalizing of actions as operations. From this point of view concrete operations may be regarded as intermediaries between actions and deductions properly so-called; formal operations are operations upon concrete operations, that is to say they are second-order operations (Inhelder and Piaget, 1958). Because the new systems formed in this way are more abstract, they permit the combination of elements from previously unrelated systems or of previously unrelated elements within systems (for instance the *INRC* group combines inversion and reciprocity; see p. 73).

One might agree with Piaget up to this point but refuse to take the next step and agree that mathematical thinking is a continuation of the process whereby formal operations derive from sensorimotor actions via concrete operations. Mathematics appears to be a new form of thinking, one too greatly reliant on language and symbolism to have arisen in this way. Piaget believes that the appearance is illusory, and that mathematical philosophers have failed to appreciate the nature of the abstractive process that gives rise to mathematical entities. It is not the usual sort of abstraction whereby, for example, one forms the concept of "green" by examining grass and other green things, for in this case "green" and "grass" are on the same plane of thinking; mathematical concepts arise by the *reflective* abstraction of which we have spoken. The essential nature of reflective abstraction is that the abstraction, when it is "reflected" on to a higher plane, constitutes a psychologically different form of thought. Essentially, though, the structures that we call "mathematical" arise in the same way as the structures of concrete and formal operations, because reflective abstraction is responsible for them all.

This point of view has three essential consequences. In the first place, Piaget is arguing that operational development is independent of both the physical characteristics of objects and the subjective characteristics of the individuals who act upon them, but arises from the actions performed by individuals upon objects; since mathematical concepts are held by Piaget to arise in the same way as operations, it follows that *mathematical truths must depend upon the laws of the co-ordination of actions (for instance, the laws describing the organization of schemata).*

Secondly, the process of reflective abstraction must lead to the freeing of form from intuitive content. Some mathematicians have pointed to the difference between classical mathematics and contemporary mathematics (which is much more abstract and less dependent upon naïve intuition*) as support for their view that mathematics has freed itself from psychological connections. If we accept Piaget's view of the construction of mathematical entities, we see that *the development of mathematics obeys the same laws as the development of operational structures.*

The final consequence of Piaget's view concerns formalization

* See Beth and Piaget (1966), ch. 5, and p. 16 of this book.

in mathematics. We have seen that operational structures have well-defined forms, and that even sensorimotor actions are organized (into schemata.) Since development proceeds by reflective abstraction, the cognitive structures of a given level of development must simultaneously be the content from which the forms of the higher levels of development will arise, and themselves be forms with respect to lower levels of development; these lower levels will also be forms with respect to yet lower levels. It follows that the distinction between form and content in intellectual structures is relative rather than absolute. A similar phenomenon can be observed in the history of mathematics, because Greek mathematics is very formal compared to Egyptian mathematics, but intuitive compared to the mathematics of the nineteenth century. *We may conclude that the elaboration of forms is not the prerogative of mathematics, but is inherent in natural thought.**

One might object to Piaget's view that mathematical formalization is the most refined type of reflective abstraction on the ground that the axioms to which formalization has led are artificial, whereas on Piaget's view one would expect them to be genetically primitive. This would be to misunderstand the situation. The mathematician, seeking axioms from which a mathematical system can be deduced, is concerned solely with validity. Reflective abstraction, on the other hand, is concerned with a factual reconstruction of intellectual structures. Inasmuch as questions of validity are not reducible to those of factual verification and *vice versa*, we must not expect the axioms discovered by formalization to correspond to genetically primitive notions discovered by reflective abstraction. Nevertheless, there is a formal similarity between the aims of the mathematician and the psychologist, because the mathematician seeks to postulate the simplest conditions from which a mathematical system can be deduced, whereas the psychologist searches for the most elementary conditions that will account for an intellectual structure. The differences between them are exaggerated by the fact that

---

* Piaget goes further and suggests that logico-mathematical entities elaborate the laws of nature.

the psychologist is concerned with *partial* reconstructions of the intellect, whilst the mathematician seeks a *complete* reconstruction of mathematics.

Another point that may be made to support the view that mathematical and natural thought are essentially similar is this. We know that it is never possible to define all axioms within the framework of the mathematical system of which they are a part, and that attempts to define them without a meta-language (i.e. concepts outside the framework in question) involve circularity of argument. The same is true of everyday language, because every word in the dictionary is defined in terms of other words in the same dictionary.

Throughout all these arguments we can trace one major theme, namely that genetic analysis of individual human development can shed light on the progress of the history of ideas. If the parallels that have been traced are as true as has been suggested, it follows that a study of the history of ideas—by the so-called "historico-critical method"—can reinforce the method of genetic analysis. Beth agrees with Piaget on this point,* but they stress that one must distinguish between the "psychological subject" (the conscious, experiencing individual) and the "epistemic subject" (that which all individuals at a given level of development have in common.) They feel that the notion of the epistemic subject has great potential value as a framework within which a series of fruitful collaborations between philosophers and psychologists can be pursued.

* Beth and Piaget (1966), "General Conclusions".

IV

PERSPECTIVE

CHAPTER 7

More about Genetic Epistemology

THE major emphasis in this book has been laid upon mathematical thinking, and there is sound justification for this. In the first place mathematical reasoning, being deductive and hence capable of attaining certainty, has often been regarded as the pinnacle of human intellectual attainment. Secondly, inasmuch as the products of mathematical activity are purely intellectual creations (any application to reality that they may have being of secondary importance, mathematically speaking) they are of especial interest to psychologists. Finally, Piaget appears to take mathematical thinking as his model of reasoning, to which all other forms of intellection are in some degree inferior.

However, it would be wrong to suppose that it is only mathematical epistemology that has occupied Piaget. In his three-volume *Introduction à l'épistémologie génétique* (Piaget, 1950), the fruit of his tenure of the Chair of the History of Scientific Thought at the University of Geneva, Piaget discusses thinking in mathematics, physics, biology, psychology, and sociology, as well as the status of formal logic as a system of axioms for intellectual operations. It is necessary at this point to give a very brief account of this very large work.

Piaget starts by expressing a view of philosophy that has since gained wide currency among philosophers, namely that it is a mistake to think of philosophy as a speciality, like the sciences. The mistake came about because the sciences made such strides once they separated themselves from philosophy and became specialized that philosophers thought that philosophy, too, must become specialized. This view has resulted in an unfortunate divorce of philosophical speculation from observation and experiment. Piaget believes that philosophy must re-establish its links with science and, moreover, that philosophy has much to gain from adopting the scientific approach. For example, geometers did not come to a conclusion about the nature of space before developing their theorems, physicists proceed successfully without having agreed upon that nature of matter, and psychologists owe much of their success to a refusal to pronounce upon the nature of the mind. Similarly, epistemologists should not wait to decide what knowledge is before undertaking a study of what is involved in knowing. The sort of question that Piaget feels that it would be fruitful for epistemologists to investigate is the manner in which scientific thinking has proceeded from a state of lesser knowledge to a state that is commonly judged to be superior. Piaget's own work has, as we have seen, been concerned with this problem within the framework of individual development.

Piaget believes that a study of the ontogenesis of ideas in the individual sheds light upon the development of scientific and mathematical thinking in the course of intellectual history, because the two types of development are parallel, just as the development of the embryo parallels the development of organisms in the course of evolutionary history.

Any study of development must choose a frame of reference towards which the development is thought of as proceeding. Piaget chooses as his frame of reference the state of scientific knowledge about the real world as it exists at the moment of analysis and the rational instruments of thinking as represented by the current state of elaboration of logic and mathematics. In so far as science and mathematics are constantly changing, so is the frame of reference to which our studies of development are related. It follows that these studies can have no theoretical termination.

Within this general framework it is possible to define differences between the sciences according the logical status of their data. Mathematics, for example, may be called "idealist", because mathematical notions are not constrained by reality: mathematical notions are constructed entirely by the intellectual activity of the mathematician. Physics is constrained by reality, but its practitioners attempt to transcend reality by their mathematical conceptualizations of the data. Biology has not yet achieved this (though biometry and mathematical eugenics may alter the picture), because biological data are intimately linked to the real world: this has the consequence that biological classification is qualitative rather than quantitative and therefore, in Piaget's terms, achieves only the status of "groupings" not "groups" (see Chapter 4). Psychology and sociology (distinguished in that psychology deals with individuals, sociology with groups) occupy a position between mathematics and biology analogous to that occupied by physics. Whereas physics attempts to be idealist but is constrained by the nature of things to be realist, psychology and sociology start by being realist but are obliged to consider the idealist products of the human beings whom they study, namely the intellectual creations that constitute the data of mathematics.

Clearly there are intimate relationships between the sciences, which create difficulties for any attempt at "reductionism". By a reductive explanation is meant an attempt to demonstrate the relationships existing within a set of concepts having certain features by reference to another set of concepts not having those features (for instance explaining human conduct and emotions by reference to neurophysiology). The problem is complicated by the fact that there are two sorts of reduction, as we shall see.

First of all, physical concepts may be reduced to mathematical concepts because there is a logical *correspondence* between the data arising from physical experiments and the mathematical notions that are used to represent these data. On the other hand, biological concepts may be reduced to physical concepts because of a relationship of *interdependence* between physical notions and the physico-chemical organisms who construct those notions. In the case of the reduction of psychological (and sociological) concepts to biological, both sorts of relationship are found: there is an interdependence of behaviour and biological mechanisms, and

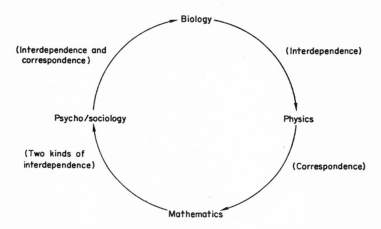

FIG. 7.1. Relationships of reduction within the circle of the sciences.

a correspondence of consciousness and physiological states (this correspondence is usually described as "psychophysical parallelism").

When we turn to the reduction of mathematical concepts to those of psychology and sociology the relationship is rather different. Two kinds of reduction are found, but they are both examples of interdependence. First, mathematics may be reduced to logic, not in the simple, straight-forward way proposed by logicians of an earlier generation, but because the notion of number arises in the individual from the interaction of the notions of class and relation (see Chapter 3). The second example may be illustrated by the attempts of mathematicians such as Poincaré to explain the origins of mathematical notions by reference to introspective awareness (see Chapters 1 and 6).

In summary we see that attempts at reductive explanation are circular, physical concepts being reducible to mathematical, mathematical concepts to those of psychology and sociology, which in turn are reducible to the concepts of physics. These relationships are displayed in Fig. 7.1.

CHAPTER 8

Piaget's Contributions to Education

PROFESSOR FLAVELL discusses three ways in which Piaget's findings may be applied to education (Flavell, 1963, pp. 365–70). In the first place they afford a means of assessing the individual student's capacity for benefiting from a programme of instruction and of diagnosing his difficulties. Secondly, they offer guidance for planning the content of the curriculum as a whole in the light of established norms of development. Finally, Piaget's findings suggest methods of teaching once the curriculum content has been decided.

In the light of these potential applications it is at first surprising to learn that Piaget's views originally encountered considerable hostility from many educators, and that, although there is less hostility today than previously there has still been no systematic attempt to apply Piaget's findings to education. Let us see if we can account for this state of affairs.

In 1964 Piaget put his views succinctly to a conference of educators, who then discussed the educational implications of these views. We shall find it instructive to look at the report of this conference.* First of all, Piaget distinguishes *development* from *learning*. Development, for Piaget, is a spontaneous process linked with the whole process of embryogenesis. Most people think of embryogenesis as concerned solely with bodily development, but Piaget maintains that we must think of it as including the development of mental functions. The essential characteristic of development is its spontaneity.

Learning, on the other hand, is not spontaneous but is provoked

* *Journal of Research in Science Teaching*, vol. 2, pp. 176–86.

by situations. Moreover, the changes brought about by learning are limited to the specific intellectual structures required to deal with the particular situations, whereas development involves the *totality* of intellectual structures.

Therefore we cannot explain development in terms of learning as, for example, the sum of discrete learning experiences. On the contrary, development is the fundamental process, and we must explain learning in terms of development, because learning occurs as a function of development.

To see why this must be so, we have to remind ourselves of the nature of an *operation*, the central concept of Piaget's system. For Piaget, knowing an object means acting on the object and mentally transforming its properties. An operation always forms part of a total intellectual structure, and this structure must exist in some form before the child is able to "operate" upon objects. Thus, before the child can know an object, he must have developed the essential intellectual structure which implies that learning is not possible until development has reached a certain level.

If learning cannot explain development, we must explain how development from one set of intellectual structures to another comes about. Piaget discusses four factors that may be responsible. They are: physical maturation; experience; social transmission; and equilibration or self-regulation. We shall consider them in turn.

There are two reasons why Piaget believes that *physical maturation* is an insufficient explanation of development. In the first place, we know little about the development of the nervous system after the child's second birthday; and in the second, intellectual structures appear at different ages in different cultures, even though the order of their appearance is constant. As examples of the phenomenon of cultural differences in the ages at which intellectual structures appear, Piaget tells us that in Teheran the ages are approximately the same as in Geneva, whilst in the villages of Iran there is a systematic delay of 2 years; Montreal has the same ages as Geneva, but in Martinique (where the French educational system and curriculum are operative) there is a 4-year delay.

There are two reasons also why *experience* is an insufficient explanation. First, some of the structures of concrete operations cannot depend upon experience. For instance, if one alters the shape of a ball of plasticine and asks a 6-year-old child if the amount of plasticine remains the same, the child will probably agree that it does; yet the same child may well deny that the weight and volume remain constant. To an adult, the child's replies seem inconsistent, because an adult will confirm the conservation of the amount of substance by checking that the weight and volume remain the same. The child's notion of conservation of substance cannot depend upon experience, because his denial of the conservation of weight and volume shows that he has not reasoned out the conservation of substance in physical terms; instead, he has "adopted" the notion as a strategy for solving problems. As Piaget puts it, the child knows that *something* must be conserved, else he could not return to the starting point, but he does not know what. Therefore, the conservation of substance becomes, for the child, a logical necessity.

The second reason why experience alone cannot account for intellectual development is that the very notion is equivocal. The term may refer to *physical* experience, which is drawn from objects (for instance weighing two objects to discover which is heavier), or to *logico-mathematical* experience. Logico-mathematical experience is drawn not from objects but from the actions that the child performs upon those objects and which "modify" those objects. For instance, a child may discover that a pile of pebbles may be put in line, and their sum is the same when they are counted from either end, or even when they are rearranged in a circle. The child has not discovered a property of pebbles, but has discovered a property of the *action of ordering*. By his actions with respect to the pebbles, the child has modified the pebbles, by setting them in order. Such actions later become interiorized as operations, and combine with other operations to form intellectual structures. Piaget regards logico-mathematical experience as considerably more significant for intellectual development than physical experience, which is probably what most people mean when they say that experience is necessary for development to occur. Clearly the notion of logico-mathematical experience is intimately bound up with Piaget's whole conception of intellectual development.

The third factor to be considered is *social transmission*. Piaget feels that social transmission cannot account for development, because a child cannot receive information by way of language, or of education directed by adults, unless he already has the intellectual structures that will permit him to assimilate the information. Once more, then, we see that it is necessary to explain learning in terms of development, rather than vice versa.

The final factor, *equilibration*, is already familiar to us from Chapters 2–5 of the present book. Knowing is an active process, and if the child is faced with novel information, he will have to react in order to compensate for the disturbance that this new information causes. To take a simple example: when a ball of plasticine is rolled into a sausage shape a 4-year-old child will say, as it gets longer, that there is more plasticine. However, there will come a point where it seems too long, and the child will say that there is *less* plasticine because it is thinner, that is to say, the focus of attention has changed from length to width. When he is a little older he will realize that the amount stays the same because, although it is longer, it is also thinner. When he is able to think in this way he has attained reversibility, because he can balance a transformation in one direction by another transformation in an opposite direction.

We may think of development as a progression through a series of stages, each characterized by an active search for equilibrium. When the equilibrium of any one stage is disturbed, the child must so accommodate himself in order to assimilate the new information that he achieves a new level of adaptation, characterized by its own form of equilibrium. The most advanced equilibrated system is that of formal operations, where *any* transformation in one direction can be balanced by a transformation in another, so no new form of equilibrium need be sought. Inasmuch as the search for equilibrium characterizes the progression through the various developmental stages to the level of formal operations, we may regard equilibration as a crucial factor in development.

So far our discussion has concerned development, an understanding of which Piaget considers vital to our appreciation of the human intellect. On the topic of learning he has rather less to say. Piaget considers the stimulus–response paradigm of classical learning theory inadequate as an explanation of learning because one defines a stimulus as something that sets off a response, and a response cannot occur unless the organism has the appropriate structure that makes the response possible. In a sense, therefore, the response must potentially exist before the stimulus. Piaget would replace the one-way S–R model with that of a schema, which is circular. The essential element in behaviour, as Piaget conceives the situation, is the structure that makes a response possible, and hence permits something to be a stimulus. Piaget's investigations have, as we know, concerned the development of the various structures.

In terms of Piaget's analysis, S–R training cannot accelerate intellectual development if this training is limited to *physical* experience, because *logico-mathematical* experience is the essential factor. To illustrate this, Piaget cites experiments done by Smedslund on the conservation of weight and the transitivity of weight.* The conservation of weight can be checked by the physical experience of weighing, but there is no way of checking that if *A* is heavier than *B* and *B* is heavier than *C*, then *A* must be heavier than *C*: transitivity is a logico-mathematical structure. Nevertheless, Smedslund ascertained from the spontaneous remarks made by children aged 5–6 years that the notions of conservation and transitivity of weight were associated. He then attempted to accelerate the understanding of weight in still younger children by giving them experience of handling and weighing plasticine cut up in various ways and made into various shapes. With these younger children Smedslund was able to accelerate the development of the notion of *conservation* of weight

* See also Smedslund, *J. Res. Sci. Teaching*, vol. 2, pp. 220–1.

but not the notion of transitivity. Piaget's explanation is that logico-mathematical structures are not amenable to checking against physical reality, and so their development cannot be accelerated by the physical experience that constitutes S–R training.

However, it *is* possible for physical experience to affect logico-mathematical experience if the physical experience and the logico-mathematical experience have the same structure. By way of illustration Piaget refers to the conservation of number. If one places a row of red counters opposite a row of blue counters so that they are in one-to-one correspondence, a young child will agree that there is the same number in each row. If he next spreads out one row, children aged less than 7 years will claim that there is no longer the same number in each row. If, on the other hand, one asks a child to take beads from a large pile and to put one with each hand into two glasses, and to continue in this way after the glasses are covered so that he cannot see where the beads are going, he will affirm that there must be the same number in each, from the age of $5\frac{1}{2}$ years.*

The reason why conservation is attained so early in the second case is that number is a synthesis of ordering and class-inclusion, and the child's action in putting the beads into the glasses, being a continuous iteration, is both ordered and inclusive. Thus the physical experience has the same structure as the logico-mathematical experience, and can facilitate its development. By suitable intermediate steps one can generalize the child's understanding to the situation where the beads are laid out in rows.

Piaget concludes that learning of intellectual structures is possible if and only if a more complex structure is based on simpler structures. S–R training will inevitably be unsuccessful because it provides only external reinforcement, whereas, since the learning of structures appears to obey the same laws as the *development* of these structures, the reinforcement must itself be in the nature of a structure. Once again Piaget is led to claim that learning is subordinate to development.

* Compare this with Frank's experiment reported in the next chapter.

The fundamental difference between Piaget's approach and the S–R approach, as Piaget conceives it, is that the S–R model is of learning by *association*, whereas Piaget holds the fundamental relation, involved in both development and learning, to be one of *assimilation*, that is to say, the integration of experience of reality into an intellectual structure. Learning, for Piaget, is active assimilation, and it is the task of pedagogy to ensure that this activity takes place on the occasions that we call "learning situations".

We may discuss Piaget's contributions from three points of view. First we can point out that Piaget misconceives the nature of contemporary learning theory. It is not true that learning theorists ignore the question of what constitutes a stimulus; much of the current research into operant learning is concerned less with responses than with discrimination. Experiments have shown that a subject's response to a situation depends upon his past experience of similar situations; which suggests that he somehow internalizes certain features of past situations, and these internalized features determine to what features of future situations he will respond.*

Piaget's reply to this point would be on the following lines. In order to accommodate the results of Piagetian-type experiments within the framework of S–R theory, one must modify the original meanings of "stimulus" and "response" to such an extent that they take on entirely different significations. Piaget's own concepts deal much more successfully with the available data on the growth of the intellect, so it would be better to adopt a Piagetian model rather than the drastically modified S–R paradigm.

Essentially the issue is this. Piaget's concepts and vocabulary are not those of the rest of psychology. To learn about Piaget's psychology one must master both Piagetian language and S–R language; this is clearly wasteful of intellectual energy, and it would be better if only one sort of language were employed. S–R theory has the advantage of being more comprehensive, and

* Ripple, *J. Res. Sci. Teaching*, vol. 2, pp. 187–95.

so it is tempting to rewrite Piaget in S–R terms. Some years ago learning theorists attempted, for precisely these reasons, to rephrase Freud (Dollard and Miller, 1950). However, Freudians and many other psychologists continue to employ Freudian vocabulary because it seems that much of the essential content of Freudianism is lost in translation into S–R terms. The same may well prove true of Piagetianism. This, then, is a methodological issue, which will only be resolved by time. Disputes about whether Piaget or the S–R theorists more correctly describe the changes that both would agree occur in learning situations do not really advance the case of either.

If the case of Piaget *versus* S–R theory is at least partly a pseudo-issue, the next point is not. It is admittedly the fact that traditional learning theory has not been the inspiration of pedagogy. Unfortunately, neither has Piaget's work, although his normative findings have caused educators to reconsider the nature of the children who are being taught. It is true that Piaget's work has been the inspiration of educational research,* but as Cronbach† points out, although educators are agreed that a child should be encouraged to discover things for himself, there is no systematic theory in terms of which a teacher can tell precisely how much free discovery, and when, should be introduced into the classroom situation. From this point of view Piaget's writings are no more helpful than S–R theory. The construction of the bridge linking psychological theory to pedagogical practice is a crucial task for educational technology.

The fact that Piaget has not been the direct inspiration of pedagogy is underlined by the third part of the conference to which we have been referring, in which a number of educators describe attempts to improve the school curriculum. What emerges most clearly from these reports is that improvements to the curriculum have come about as a result of the analysis of the structure of the

---

* For example Bruner (1960), Dienes (1960), Lovell, (1961), Lunzer (1962), Peel (1960), and a series of booklets published by the National Froebel Foundation.

† *J. Res. Sci. Teaching*, vol. 2, pp. 204–7.

material to be taught. This brings us to the third point of criticism of Piaget's views, namely that many educators are not convinced that learning is as unimportant as Piaget suggests.

The view that they take is that Piaget is an observer, not a teacher, and what he observes is the understanding that children have, at different ages, when they have been taught in conventional ways. If teachers adopt new methods they may alter the data of Piaget's research, even to the extent of modifying the order of emergence of the various stages.*

The role of teaching in the development of the intellect is discussed concisely by Nathan Isaacs.† He points out that Piaget's earlier work was severely criticized by educationists on the gounds that it relied too much on verbal questioning of children, with results that appeared to go directly counter to the aims of progressive education. Although Piaget's findings are now accepted, having been confirmed by observations in practical situations, the basic issue of mental maturation *versus* educational experience remains. The cumulative effect of Piaget's work has confirmed the initial picture of an inward evolution, whereas progressive educationists can point to changes in the ways in which young children understand reality, apparently resulting from advanced educational techniques.

Isaacs suggests that an examination of adult thinking may help to resolve the dilemma. Adults normally function at the level of formal operations with respect to logic, causal thinking, and so on, but emotional involvement, anxiety, and so on, may cause a regression to a less sophisticated level. For instance,‡ to the question "Do you weigh more after a meal than before?" more women than men will be inclined to answer "No". Isaacs' point is that we only function at our best in the most favourable circumstances. The same is probably true of children, and it may be that Piagetian-type experimental situations provide less favourable

* Kilpatrick, *J. Res. Sci. Teaching*, vol. 2, pp. 247–51.
† See National Froebel Foundation booklet *Some Aspects of Piaget's Work*.
‡ This is not Isaacs' example, but was suggested to the present author by Dr. Adam Bardecki, of the Manor Hospital, Epsom.

circumstances than the teaching situations devised by progressive educationists. Moreover, when a child is observed by Piaget, his past experience may not have comprised uniformly favourable circumstances, and so even if the child were at his best when observed by Piaget, his performance would inevitably show the effect of unfavourable past experiences. Isaacs, then, is not adopting the extremely critical view of the teachers quoted by Kilpatrick,* but is attempting a resolution of the conflict between Piaget and progressive educators.

There is another issue between Piaget and the teachers, namely that Piaget maintains that the major, if not the only, forces determining progression towards the adult level of thinking are the processes of *socialization*, that is to say free discussion and peer-group interaction. Isaacs accepts the importance of socialization, but insists that there are other forces which depend upon the right social conditions but make their own contribution. He feels that one must insist on the importance of these forces if one is to account for the fact that not all societies achieve the same level of mental functioning, even though the process of socialization is necessary in all of them. These processes are: discovering; testing; making and planning. In societies where the educational system does not actively encourage these processes, intellectual growth may be reduced to the minimum. Isaacs feels that the levels of conceptual functioning described by Piaget may represent something like this minimum.

Isaacs feels that Piaget's central concept of operation has much to offer the progressive educator. In the light of Piaget's analysis of intellectual growth as the accumulation of operational thought proceeding through a number of well-defined stages, the teacher can devise situations that most efficiently foster the advance through these stages. The teacher must understand the children whom he teaches before he can teach effectively. Piaget's work affords, in the opinion of Isaacs and many other educationists, the best model yet constructed to facilitate this understanding.

* *J. Res. Sci. Teaching*, vol. 2, pp. 247–51.

Now that we have reviewed some of Piaget's indirect contributions to education (indirect, inevitably, because Piaget is a research scientist, not an educator) let us return to Flavell's three suggested applications. The first was that Piaget's findings afford a means of assessment of the individual learner's difficulties. Piaget himself has not been much concerned with this aspect of psychology, but a number of his followers have attempted to construct tests.* These tests have so far been applied more in the field of the education of subnormal children and adults rather than average or above average individuals (see Woodward, 1959), although attempts are being made to incorporate Piagetian items into tests for the general population (see Warburton, 1966).

The reason why Piagetian assessment methods have not up till now been widely applied in the educational field is that there is necessarily an intimate connection between an educational system and the types of test that are employed in connection with that system. The necessity arises from the fact that a test must be valid, that is to say, the predictions that one makes on the basis of the test scores must to a certain extent be confirmed: inevitably, tests are refined in use so that they are more efficient prediction devices, which in practice means that the tests employed in education are modified so as to relate ever more closely to the educational system.† Inasmuch as Piaget's findings have not greatly affected conventional education (particularly at the secondary level), Piagetian-type tests find little educational application.

We have already seen the reason why Piaget has not had a greater impact upon education, namely that his findings were initially presented in such a way as to arouse hostility among precisely those educators who were most likely to apply new ideas; and, taken at their face value, they still appear antithetical to teaching. One might hope that in the near future the conflict would be resolved so that Flavell's other suggested

* For example Pinard and Laurendeau, *J. Res. Sci. Teaching*, vol. 2, pp. 253–60.

† See any sound text in psychometrics, e.g. Vernon (1960, 1964).

applications—guidance for planning curriculum content and guidance in methods of teaching—might become actual rather than potential.

Before this could happen, however, a peaceful revolution in education would be necessary. Many educators feel that the history of education from Froebel onwards has been continuing revolution resulting in the emancipation of the child from the drudgery of mastering "learning" imposed from outside, and freeing him to discover for himself the world of reality and his own place in it. If Piaget's work contributes to yet greater emancipation of the child, Piaget will be seen, by posterity, to have been in the great tradition of educational reformers.

CHAPTER 9

Language and Cognitive Development

THIS chapter is concerned with two topics which have in common
the theme of language. The first topic is Piaget's early work on
children's language and thinking and the criticisms that it
encountered, particularly from Russian psychologists: the second
is the controversy between the schools of Geneva and Harvard
over the role of language in cognitive growth.

Piaget's early work on child language, first published in English
in 1926 (Piaget, 1959), was designed to discover the needs that a
child satisfies when he talks. The theme of the investigation was
that the child's language expresses his intellectual structure;
the language that Piaget observed was that used by children,
aged between 4 and 11 years, in their conversations with each
other and with adults. Piaget classified children's utterances (and
hence their thinking) as either *egocentric* or *socialized*, meaning by
"egocentric" that the child behaves and talks as if all points
of view were identical to his own; egocentric thinking is characterized by *syncretism*, that is to say, the tendency to assimilate any
features of reality whatsoever into undifferentiated intellectual
schemata. Egocentrism is a transitional stage between the autism
of the earliest years, when the child's life is one of self-satisfying
fantasy, and the social adaptation of later years. The proportion
of childish utterances that may be classified as egocentric declines
slowly from an average of 51 per cent at 3 years of age to 45
per cent at 6 years, and then dramatically to 28 per cent at 7.
The increase in the socialized component comes about as a result
of interactions with other children (and to a lesser extent with

adults), which oblige the child to accommodate his point of view to theirs.

The age of 7, when egocentrism suffers a marked decline, is the age at which the structures of concrete operations start to appear. This is no coincidence. Egocentrism characterizes the period when the individual's actions are centred upon his own personality and are not otherwise co-ordinated; operational systems are the expressions of co-ordinated actions which by their very nature imply taking account of the viewpoints of other people. Operational systems are therefore characterized by co-operation between individuals and co-ordination within the individual, and this double mechanism of adjustment frees the individual from his initial egocentrism.*

Piaget's account met with considerable opposition, particularly from investigators in Britain and the United States, who objected that the amount of egocentrism in the child's language had been exaggerated by Piaget. Piaget (1959, ch. 6) replied to many of these criticisms by pointing out that many of his critics had paid too much attention to the superficial aspects of the utterances (for instance, the use of "I" or "me"), when they should have examined the utterances to see whether they were genuine attempts at communication rather than an expression of a personal viewpoint which recognized no other. He adduced new evidence for egocentrism in this sense. In particular he showed that the proportion of egocentrism in children's utterances to adults is greater than in their utterances to other children. The reason for the difference appears to be that most exchanges between adults and children consist of questions by the child and answers by the adult, whereas children talking to each other are more likely to volunteer spontaneous information.

Piaget points out that children whose development is forced beyond the limits of natural spontaneity may parade their knowledge before adults, and in this way the proportion of egocentrism in their speech may be artificially low. In the normal course of

* This formulation, found in the 1959 edition of *Language and Thought*, is more recent than the first edition of the book.

events, however, the young child regards the adult as a superior being, a source of information rather than someone with whom he can hold a discussion. As he grows older he loses his feeling of relative inferiority and is able to converse with adults as well as with children. The essential point is that the child's intellectual structure changes as he grows older, and the change is reflected in his language; investigators must, however, ensure that the utterances they record are true reflections of the underlying intellectual structure.

Piaget recognizes that the choice of the term "egocentrism" was unfortunate in that its connotations have given rise to interpretations that he did not intend. Much of the research based on this concept has, therefore, been less fruitful than it might have been, and Piaget suggests that a more substantial basis for research might be an analysis of mental operations (Vygotsky, 1962, ch. 2).

Another line of criticism came from the Soviet Union, where Vygotsky wrote the preface to the Russian edition of Piaget's work. This criticism has only recently been translated into English (Piaget, 1959, p. 281). Vygotsky raised three major objections to Piaget's interpretation of his data.

In the first place he showed that the child's language is in certain situations intimately associated with his actions, and urged that the connection should be examined more closely. For instance, a child of $5\frac{1}{2}$ was drawing a picture of a bus when the point of his pencil broke. After trying unsuccessfully to complete the drawing with the broken pencil the child muttered "It's broken", discarded the pencil in favour of paints and paintbrush, and then proceeded to depict a *broken* bus after an accident. The frustration that occurred during the drawing provoked an egocentric utterance, which manifestly affected his subsequent activity.*

Vygotsky's second point is that the "internal speech" of adults is essentially egocentric, so egocentrism does not simply atrophy

* Many more examples of the regulation of behaviour by speech are described by Vygotsky's student Luria (1961).

with age as Piaget suggests. Piaget would object that the intellectual makeup of the adult is so different from that of the child that it would be misleading to apply the term "egocentric" to adult thought, but Vygotsky's point suggests we may distinguish two modes of thinking in adults as against one in children. The mechanism of internal speech begins to be stabilized at around 7 years of age, shortly after the child starts to attend school.

The third point is closely related to the second, but concerns a different conceptualization of the functions of speech. According to Vygotsky, all speech is social in intent inasmuch as it is intended as a form of conduct with others, but it is not necessarily communicative. Vygotsky's scheme therefore proposes that the direction of speech is from social to egocentric rather than the other way. Egocentric speech, in Vygotsky's formulation, arises when the child starts conversing with himself. This criticism may appear to be a verbal quibble, with Vygotsky's term "communicative speech" substituted for Piaget's "socialized speech", but the argument has more substance than this. In Vygotsky's scheme internal speech, which is egocentric in character, serves both autistic and logical functions, whereas Piaget regards egocentrism as a transitional stage between autistic and logical thinking.*

Vygotsky's criticism goes even further, and rejects the view that autistic thinking is a primitive stage in the genesis of thought. Instead, autistic thought is regarded as a late development, made possible by the elaboration of realistic, conceptual thinking, which permits a separation of fantasy from reality. (In taking this view Vygotsky was, of course, also opposing the Freudian view of the progression from the pleasure principle to the reality principle.)†

We have already seen that Piaget now proposes that we should pay less attention to egocentrism as a factor in development and

* Vygotsky further discusses his views on egocentric and inner speech in chapter 4 of his book.

† See any sound account of Freud, e.g. Brown (1961), ch. 1; Hall and Lindzey (1957), ch. 2.

concentrate rather on the development of groupings, so many of Vygotsky's criticisms no longer apply.* However, Vygotsky's views are sufficiently important in their own right to require mention. There is, moreover, another feature of the Russian approach, which is relevant to the topic of our previous chapter, namely education.

The point concerns the inevitability of intellectual development. Piaget, as we know, believes that social factors, whilst they exert an important influence on the growth of the intellect, are not crucial. The Soviet view, expressed by both Vygotsky (1962, ch. 6) and Luria (1961, ch. 1), is that mental activities are conditioned from the outset by social relationships. Luria adduces considerable experimental evidence to support the view that social contacts, largely through speech, give the child new ways to organize his mental activities. Moreover, the internalization of speech, which characterizes nearly all higher forms of mental activity, can often be advanced to before the seventh year by suitable contacts with adults, that is to say, by training.

The fact that intellectual development can in some cases be advanced by training leads to an important suggestion, first made by Vygotsky and reiterated by Luria, that the level of a child's intellectual development should be assessed in terms of what he can do given adult help. Two 8-year-olds may both be able to solve, without help, problems designed for 8-year-olds, making them both appear to be intellectually average. With help, one may be able to solve problems designed for 12-year-olds, whilst the other may be unable to advance beyond the 9-year-old level. Clearly the former child would be superior. It is admitted that a child must have attained a certain developmental level before he can benefit from adult assistance, but the fact that children differ in their ability to make use of adult help suggests that the conventional ways of assessing intellectual development in children, which do not take account of this differential ability, give an incomplete and misleading picture of mental growth.

* See Piaget (1962) for his comments on Vygotsky's criticisms.

Let us now turn to the current research on the role of language in cognitive growth and the differences between the Harvard school, represented by Professor Bruner, and the Geneva school of Piaget, Professor Inhelder, and their associates. First we shall give an account of Bruner's view on the course of cognitive growth (Bruner, 1964; Bruner *et al.*, 1966).

Bruner believes that the human intellect is shaped by a series of advances in the way in which the mind is used; like Piaget, he sees a parallel between individual development and the development of the human race. Bruner is concerned with two major problems: first, the ways in which human beings represent to themselves the recurrent regularities in their environment; secondly, the ways in which acts (both physical and mental) are integrated into higher-order assemblies, which make it possible to employ increasingly large units of information in solving problems.

The course of evolution appears to have been influenced by man's increasing use of systems to implement his actions. These systems are of three kinds: first, amplifiers of motor capacities (tools, for example); second, amplifiers of sensory capacities (for instance signalling systems); third, amplifiers of ratiocinative capacities (e.g., language systems). To be effective, an implementing system must be linked to an appropriate skill. The skills corresponding to the three implementing systems are, respectively: the ability to organize sensorimotor acts; the ability to organize percepts; and the ability to organize thoughts. These skills, which have been selected in the course of evolution, are precisely those that are required for representing regularities in the environment.

Bruner labels these ways of representing regularities *enactive*, *iconic*, and *symbolic* respectively. The enactive mode represents events by appropriate motor responses; for instance, normally we find our way about a familiar environment without the aid of mental images because our muscles have developed appropriate ways of responding. Iconic representation, on the other hand, selectively organizes percepts and images to construct a "picture" of the world. Finally, symbolic representation employs symbols that need in no way resemble the things that they refer to; words, for instance, do not look, and seldom sound, like the things that they describe. These three modes of representation develop in the child in that order, and the characteristic feature of the progression is an increase in the remoteness of the mode of representation from the thing represented. Bruner's work has been mainly concerned with the transition from iconic to symbolic representation, which starts at about 4 years of age.

The child shows the beginnings of symbolic representation in the second year of life, when his language comprises mainly *holophrases*, that is to say, one-word sentences. Shortly after this, two classes of words appear, a *pivot class* (for example "allgone") and an *open class* (for instance, "bye-bye", "sticky"). The child is able to construct more sophisticated sentences with these two classes. When a visitor has left he may say "all gone bye-bye"; after his mother has washed jam from his hands he may say "allgone sticky".

From these simple references to events, the child goes on to construct a language system that does more than just describe reality: it transforms it. We may express one and the same event in three different ways for different purposes. For example, we may say "*X* did *A* to *Y*", "*A* was done to *Y* by *X*", "Wasn't *A* done to *Y* by *X*?" It is this transforming function of language that has been singled out by linguists as its most important feature (see Chomsky in (ed.) Saporta, 1961).

From the point of view of young children preparing, in Piaget's terms, for the phase of concrete operations, (i.e. children aged from 4 to 7 years) a crucial feature is the ability to use language to order experiences by describing things as having more or less of a given property. Bruner describes a number of experiments that illustrate the confusions that children suffer in the time of transition from iconic to symbolic representation.

In one experiment, children aged between 5 and 7 years were shown nine glasses set out in matrix form on a large piece of cardboard, as in Figure 9.1. The children were asked to describe the matrix and say how the glasses were alike and how they differed. Then the matrix was scrambled and the children were asked to replace the glasses on the cardboard "to make something like what was there before". Nearly all the children succeeded in this, the only difference between younger and older children being that the older children were quicker. Then the matrix was scrambled once more, but the glass marked *A* in Fig. 9.1 was placed in the spot marked *X*, and the child was asked to build something like the original matrix, leaving the glass in

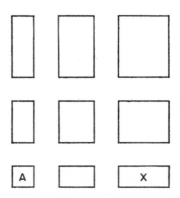

FIG. 9.1. Matrix of glasses used in Bruner's transposition task (modified from Bruner, 1964).

its new position. This time, most of the 7-year-olds succeeded, whilst the 5's and 6's failed.

Examination of the language used by the children showed that it was closely related to success or failure on the reconstruction task. The younger children appeared to be dominated by a visual image of the original matrix, whereas the older children were able to talk to themselves about the problem and thus take account of the physical transformation.

The ability to employ language instrumentally in this way depended upon the terms used by children in their descriptions

of the original matrix. Bruner distinguishes three so
criptions, namely *dimensional*, *global*, and *confounded*. In di\
descriptions, the two ends of an attribute are singled ͺ
"that one is higher and that one is shorter"). A global desc
can apply to any attribute (for instance "that one is big an\
one is little"). In confounded usage, a dimensional term is ᵤsed
for one end of an attribute, a global term for the other ("that
one is taller and that one is little").* Children who employed
confounded descriptions were most likely to fail on the transposition task, but the children's language was in no way related
to their performance on the *untransposed* matrix.

We have already said that the younger children appeared
to be dominated by an image of the original matrix or, to put it
more formally in Bruner's terms, they were over-influenced by
iconic representation. The question arises whether a child's
performance could be improved if one helped him to make use
of his existing language habits. Luria, as we have seen earlier in
this chapter, has reported that even very young children (3
years old) can be assisted in discrimination tasks by a directed
integration of speech and action, but Bruner's work concerns not
discrimination but conceptual understanding. The experiment
about to be reported investigates the possibility that having the
child "describe" an event in the absence of the event to be described, can help to overcome the dominance of iconic representation, and thus assist the child to attain a given level of conceptualization earlier than would normally be the case.

Piaget's experiments on conservation have shown that a young
child will say that the amount of water in a beaker changes if it
is poured into either a wider or a shallower vessel. Frank (see
Bruner, 1964) presented children aged 4, 5, 6, and 7 years with
two identical, partly-filled beakers, which the children agreed
contained the same amount of liquid. She then set a wider beaker
of the same height next to the original beakers, and placed before
all three a screen that exposed only the tops of the vessels. Frank
then poured the contents of one of the original beakers into the

* The original appears to have printing errors at these points.

wider beaker, and the child was asked to say which vessel now "had the more to drink", the wider one or the narrower one, or whether they had the same (the screen, of course, prevented the child from seeing the water levels).

In the unscreened condition, as Frank confirmed by a pre-test, children tend to say that the wider beaker has less water because the level is lower. Screening increased the number of correct judgements from 0–50 per cent among the 4-year-olds; 20–90 per cent among the 5-year-olds; and 50–100 per cent among the 6's and 7's.

An important age difference was revealed when the screen was removed. The 4-year-olds were overwhelmed by the visual display, and they all changed their minds. Most of the 5-year-olds, and all the older children, maintained their judgement of equality.

Some minutes later Frank repeated the experiment, this time without using a screen, to see if there had been a transfer effect. She found that there had, as 70 per cent of the 5-year-olds and 90 per cent of the 6- and 7-year-olds judged that the amount of water remained the same (as against 20 per cent and 50 per cent respectively in the pre-test conditon). From this experiment and others, Bruner concludes that a child must have an internalized verbal formula to shield him from the overwhelming effect of visual displays if he is to succeed in conservation tasks.*

Other experiments described by Bruner concern the growth of the power of classification. Children were asked to sort words or pictures into groups that were alike in some way. Bruner distinguishes two aspects of grouping as *criterion attribute* and *syntactical structure*. Three types of criterion attribute were employed by the children, namely perceptual features; arbitrary functional features (what the child can do with things irrespective of their proper function, for example "a book and a newspaper are alike because I can hit people with both of them"); and appropriate functional features ("a book and a newspaper both provide information"). Syntactical structures may be complexive (more

* We shall discuss this experiment at the end of this chapter.

than one rule is invoked in order to justify a grouping, for instance "a peach and a potato are alike because they are round, and potato and spinach are alike because I don't like them") or hierarchical (objects are arranged in relations of subordinate to superordinate, for example "peach, potato and spinach are all foodstuffs"). A study of the classifications offered by children from 6 to 19 years of age showed that 6-year-olds employ a large percentage of complexive syntactical structures (about 50 per cent) and rely on perceptual attributes, whereas 19-year-olds employ exclusively hierarchical structures and group according to appropriate functional features.

This experiment and others strengthen Bruner's contention that a crucial factor in intellectual growth is the development of hierarchical structures with rules for including objects in superordinate categories. This development takes place at the expense of perceptual groupings as language becomes progressively internalized to form a symbol system, permitting the individual to transform reality in ways that greatly increase the possible range of problem-solving techniques. The study of grouping illustrates the role of egocentrism in this development, because the child's use of arbitrary functional features (what *he* can do with objects) is a transitional stage between the reliance on perceptual attributes and classification by rules that are syntactical rather than associative.*

The characteristic feature of the Harvard school is its concern with *function*. Bruner wants to investigate the progressive ways in which the mind is used. By contrast the Geneva school (which is, of course, that of Piaget and his disciples) concerns itself with the progressive series of intellectual *structures*. This has been illustrated so often already in this book that it scarcely needs emphasizing here. However, the differences between Geneva and Harvard account for differences in both their interpretations of experimental results and the sorts of experiments that they conduct.

* This description of intellectual growth applies to children in Western culture. In other cultures the course of intellectual growth is rather different. See Bruner *et al.*, chs. 12, 13, and 14.

It is with the latter that we are primarily concerned, and in particular with experiments on the role of language in mental development reported by Inhelder *et al.* (1966).

The purpose of the experiments was to investigate the transition from the pre-operational phase to the phase of concrete operations, with particular reference to the concept of conservation. Briefly, the idea was to confront the child with the discrepancy between the outcome of a conservation problem and his predicted outcome in order to force him to reason about the discrepancy and justify his reasoning. Therefore, unlike Bruner, the Geneva experimenters did not mask those perceptual aspects of the situation that caused the child confusion, because to do so would have shielded the child from precisely those conflicts about which they wanted him to reason.

In some of their experiments Inhelder and her associates investigated the effect of language training on the child's reasoning. By means of appropriate tests they distinguished children who had the concept of conservation ("conservers") from those that had not ("non-conservers"). They then put all the children in experimental situations where they were asked to describe differences between dolls having more or fewer marbles, of different sizes, and pencils differing in length and thickness. They discovered three ways in which the linguistic expressions employed by conservers differed from those used by non-conservers.

First, the conservers used *relational terms*: for example "one has more than the other". Secondly, they employed *differentiated terms*: for instance a conserver would use two different terms (such as "long" and "fat") to describe pencils differing in both length and thickness, whereas a non-conserver would use the same term, or synonymous terms ("big", "large") for both dimensions. Thirdly, conservers employed *co-ordinated descriptives*: thus a conserver asked to describe the difference between a doll with two large marbles and another with four small ones, would say "that one has less but they're bigger"; whereas a non-conserver would centre on the two attributes successively and say "that one has a lot, and that one has a little, that one's got little ones and that one's got big ones".

Having elucidated these differences, the experimenter trained the non-conservers in the use of the appropriate linguistic expressions, then administered further conservation tests to see if the training had improved understanding. They found that children who had shown a partial understanding of conservation on the pre-tests expressed themselves more consistently and clearly on the post-tests. The previous non-conservers, who had, of course, based their pre-test judgements on water level, now spontaneously mentioned both height and width, and even compensation ("it's gone lower but it's spread out"). However, they still had not acquired the notion of conservation, because these children would remark that in one glass the level was high because the glass was thin, whereas in the other glass it was low because the glass was fat, but still insist that there was less to drink in the wide glass.*

In conclusion, the Geneva workers point out that, whilst language may assist the selection, storage, and retrieval of environmental information, it cannot aid its *co-ordination*. Co-ordination, at least in the phase of concrete operations, pre-supposes the development, by assimilation and accommodation, of the relevant intellectual structures. This is not to say that language may not make an important contribution to the structures of the phase of *formal* operations (where we may expect symbolism to play a more important role): the argument of the Geneva school is that language is insufficient to explain the initial formation of operations.

We have seen that Piaget and his co-workers regard language as a means of expressing thought, whereas Bruner considers language to be a vital technique in the development of thinking. The views of the Russian school, particularly as developed by Luria, are even more extremely opposed to Piaget's because

* Bruner found that *none* of forty children, who were asked to justify their concepts of conservation, referred to compensation. See Bruner (1964).

Russian psychologists often talk as if thought presupposes language. This cannot be the whole picture, however, because there is evidence to show that, on non-verbal tests of intelligence, the performance of deaf children does not differ much from that of children with normal hearing, a finding that is more consonant with the Geneva viewpoint (Furth, 1966).

To conclude this chapter we shall briefly discuss Frank's results with the screened conservation test from Piaget's point of view in order to show how the views of Harvard and Geneva are related.

Frank found that, when the vessels were screened, 50 per cent of the 4-year-olds said that the amounts of liquid were the same, 90 per cent of the 5-year-olds, and 100 per cent of the 6- and 7-year-olds. To say, as Bruner does, that improved performance resulted from the removal of the perceptual stimulation, fails to account for the improvements from none, 20 per cent, and 50 per cent respectively. All that this explains is why the children no longer made the *incorrect* judgement: it does not explain why they made the correct judgement. We have to suppose that the capacity for making the correct judgement was there in latent form, but that an incorrect mode of dealing with environmental information presented its appearance. This appears to be what Inhelder and her associates mean by saying that one must be careful to distinguish the actualizing of existing structures from the formation of new operational structures.

In the light of this analysis we may say that the views of Geneva and Harvard are both correct, but in different ways, Piaget accounting for the development of mental structures, Bruner for their manifestation.

Although Inhelder and her associates do not employ this particular example in their discussion of the Harvard work, it is this sort of issue that they appear to have in mind when they say that the Harvard and Geneva schools are complementary. They are surely correct in saying that further confrontation and discussion would be extremely fruitful.

CHAPTER 10

Some Points of Criticism

THE purpose of this final chapter is not to attempt a comprehensive critique of Piaget's methods and theories but to indicate some of the objections that have been raised or may be raised to Piaget's work. For this purpose we may consider Piaget's contributions as falling into three major areas: the psychological, the logico-epistemological, and the general conceptual. These distinctions are made largely for convenience, as the work must be thought of as a whole, not in parts.

With respect to the psychological contributions, Piaget has produced a very useful model in the notion of assimilation and accommodation constituting two aspects of adaptation. This is a general model of thinking, and is independent of the concept of stage. The notion of stages in development, with the mass of empirical research on stage-related behaviour, is another contribution.

The concept of stage has encountered many objections: for example, that it gives the false impression that development proceeds by a series of abrupt jerks rather than smoothly; that intellectual functioning at any one age shows more fluctuation than the concept of stage would suggest; that cross-cultural variability limits the usefulness of the concept; that environment is more influential than Piaget allows; and so on. These objections have been discussed by Ausubel,* who points out that they make unwarranted assumptions about the nature of stages. All that the

* *J. Res. Sci. Teaching*, vol. 2, pp. 261–6.

concept of stage implies is the occurrence of qualitative distinctions in modes of cognitive functioning and their appearance in an identifiable sequence in development. It does not require that transitions between stages be abrupt, nor does it imply that environment is of no importance. As for the variations in intellectual functioning at any one stage, it is true that the transition from one mode of thinking to another can occur at different times in different subject areas, but it is nevertheless possible to designate an individual as being at a given level on the basis of his overall functioning.

There is, however, a more general objection that is raised by some against Piaget's work, namely that the whole concept of stage-linked development is opposed to the general spirit informing psychological research. We saw in the previous chapter of this book that Piaget's approach to problems of development is structural, whereas Bruner's is functional, and it is fair to say that the functional approach is, on the whole, more acceptable to psychologists in general. However, it would be wrong to suppose that an approach is to be discounted if it is opposed to the *Zeitgeist*: it may, for that very reason, be extremely valuable. Indeed, as Flavell points out, the findings of ethology, and the evidence from animal studies for the existence of "critical periods" in development,* are helping to reinstate the notion of stage as a viable psychological concept.

A stronger objection to Piaget's work has been that it has not always satisfied the requirements of scientific research. Piaget's samples are small, there is seldom evidence that they adequately represent the populations from which they are drawn, statistical analysis is meagre if not entirely absent from the experimental reports, and the reports themselves do not always provide sufficient information to enable other investigators to follow exactly what has gone on. Sometimes, indeed, it appears that not all subjects of the same experiment have been subjected to the same experimental conditions, so that, in effect, Piaget conflates a number of pilot studies into one "experiment". In short, it can

* See Mink, *J. Res. Sci. Teaching*, vol. 2, pp. 196–203.

be said of Piaget, as it was often said of the Gestalt psychologists, that he conducts his experiments to illustrate his point of view rather than to gain new knowledge.

Piaget's point of view is extremely interesting, and is relevant to both the logico-epistemological and the general conceptual contributions of his work. The view is, as we have seen, that intellectual development proceeds through a series of mental structures, arising in the first instance from the child's actions upon the world around him; and this development may be described in terms of logic. Within the purview of this general approach, Piaget has inspired the collaborative efforts of many psychologists, logicians, and epistemologists.

Mays (1954) has discussed Piaget's work from the philosopher's viewpoint and concludes that the work may shed light on one of the fundamental problems of epistemology, namely the nature of thinking. Philosophers have all too often considered only adult thinking and have decided that the process is not amenable to analysis. Consideration of how the process of thinking develops in the child may offer valuable insights.

Whilst Piaget's psychology may illuminate some of the problems of philosophy, not everyone has found his philosophy to illuminate psychology. Undoubtedly part of the reason for this is the appallingly infelicitous style of presentation, but a larger part is constituted by the nature of Piaget's logical model of thinking. The purpose of a model is to facilitate conceptual grasp of a subject. It fails to do this if the amount of effort required to master the model is excessive. Many people feel that symbolic logic is an excessively difficult model, and Parsons (1960) appears to suggest that even Piaget himself has failed entirely to master its complexities. Bruner (1959) feels that the model is useful but limited, and the extensions that he suggests reveal the limitations of Piaget's general approach.

Bruner maintains that the concepts in Piaget's system are unnecessarily static, particularly the concept of equilibrium. This notion explains too much rather than too little: for instance the phase of concrete operations attains an equilibrium, but over a narrow range, so the child is compelled to move towards the more complete equilibrium of the phase of formal operations. Precisely how this transition comes about is not readily explicable in terms of equilibrium itself. Bruner characterizes Piaget's system by saying that it is concerned with the tactics of development and must be completed by reference to strategies; these strategies, he proposes, must be related to the vicissitudes of the individual's attempts to cope with environmental demands. The baby is permitted to behave in a sensorimotor fashion in a sense that the pre-school child is not; the pre-school child is obliged to converse with adults, and when he goes to school the child must attempt to understand simple physical and mechanical laws; until adolescence he may be permitted to solve his problems by reference to objects, but thereafter his teachers require him to deal with problems symbolically. Demands of this sort, Bruner argues, oblige the child to develop new tactics for coping.

Bruner is asking for external reference for Piaget's concepts, whereas Piaget is content with internal consistency as a criterion of the validity of his system. This is the crucial feature of Piaget's system that makes it so repugnant to many scientists. Science is essentially inductive. It relies on empirical evidence and cannot, therefore, be self-contained. Piaget's system attempts to give a self-contained account of development, and it is for this reason that Piaget considers a logico-mathematical model to be appropriate. This approach has more in common with a metaphysical attempt to come to grips with "the nature of things" than with the approach of modern science.

It is worth devoting a little time to a consideration of the metaphysical aspect of Piaget's system because, if this is not understood, then neither will be many features of Piaget's approach to his data. Many of Piaget's books have been published in scientific series, which has led many critics to fasten on to the unscientific aspect of the work that has already been mentioned, namely the smallness of the samples, absence of statistical analysis, incompleteness of experimental reporting and, above all, the attempt to construct an enclosed system, deriving its validity from internal consistency, rather than an open system, capable of being checked against external reality. If we cease to regard Piaget's work as scientific, many of these criticisms lose their force; criticisms of another sort become more relevant.

Piaget's work may be characterized as a neo-Aristotelian metaphysic, that is to say a metaphysical system owing many of its characteristic features to the Aristotelian ethos of European thought. The feature of Piaget's work in which the Aristotelian influence is most clearly revealed is the emphasis on man as a rational creature, unable to avoid his essential rationality because it is in his nature to be rational. Indeed, the "epistemic subject" (Beth and Piaget, 1966, ch. 12) is an almost perfect example of an Aristotelian essence. Piaget believes, moreover, that it is the nature of things that a fully rational creature should emerge in the course of evolution. Although Piaget does not specifically state this postulate, it is implied in his argument that the higher mental functions arise by reflective abstraction ultimately from sensorimotor actions; and that sensorimotor actions reflect the structure of the central nervous system, which is itself a "reflection" of the structure of DNA and RNA (Piaget and Inhelder, 1968 Preface *et passim*).

The fact that a system is metaphysical rather than scientific does not make it irrelevant to science. It does mean, however, that many of the characteristic features of science will be absent. Part of the difficulty of following Piaget's work arises from the fact that he himself appears to believe that he is being scientific when in fact he is not, as when he talks of "experiments" which, as we have already mentioned, are frequently little more than illustrations of a point of view. This failing is very serious in Piaget's case, because the system of thought that he wishes to erect is vast, and his misdescription of the basis on which he wishes to found it as experimental, rather than philosophical, arouses both confusion and hostility.

Whilst a metaphysical system can shed light on scientific problems, a metaphysical analysis of a problem cannot be substituted for a scientific analysis, because the aims of science and metaphysics are so different. A good illustration of this point is afforded by the latest work of Piaget and Inhelder. In *Mémoire et intelligence* it is argued that the cognitive organizations that arise in the course of development are self-conserving, and that their conservation constitutes a form of memory. The details of the argument need not detain us, but the essential point to grasp is that when the organized intellect operates on present material it exhibits intelligence: when it operates on the past (represented by memory images) it exhibits memory. Thus memory and intelligence are two names for what is essentially the same process. Superficially this seems to be a scientific argument, because scientific progress is often made when disparate fields of study become synthesized into one. In fact, this is pseudo-science because it is a pseudo-synthesis.

A truly scientific synthesis requires either that new experiments demonstrate that two variables previously believed to be different are the same because they have indistinguishable effects; or that a set of equations be developed to link two fields of study, as happened in the nineteenth century in the case of magnetism and electricity. Neither condition is met by Piaget and Inhelder: although they report experiments they state that these are less important than the theoretical discussion; and in place of theorems they offer the by now familiar scheme of the development of operations. No convincing reason is given as to why we should adopt Piaget's scheme in this instance, and to do so would, in fact, confuse rather than help. Scientists define their concepts where possible by reference to the data of experiments and demonstrations, and the data that psychologists use to define memory are not those that they use to define intelligence. To a great extent the difference lies precisely in the fact that the former refer to the past, the latter to the present and future. When Piaget and Inhelder propose that this distinction does not matter they reveal, for all their erudition, a lamentable lack of grasp of the nature of scientific methods.

So far in this chapter we have considered how satisfactorily

Piaget's system accomplishes what it sets out to do, which is to describe the development, in the normal individual, of logical, mathematical, and scientific concepts, and to give some account of the status of psychological data *vis-à-vis* the data of other sciences. Now we must mention things that Piaget does not treat, the non-treatment of which makes his work to that extent incomplete.

The first is the non-cognitive side of mental development. Although Piaget has written on the topics of morals (1932) and dreams (1951), he has been relatively unconcerned with personality as most psychologists conceive of it. Indeed, Piaget sometimes gives the impression that he thinks of intellectual development as comprising personality, whereas most people would regard the relationship as being the other way about. For this reason his account of development needs to be integrated with other developmental theories if it is to yield a satisfying account of normal growth. Once such integration has been attempted by Maier (1965).

The second deficiency of Piaget's system is its failure to deal with non-mathematical, non-logical, and non-scientific thinking. Piaget appears to believe that the type of thinking in which he is interested is the only valid type, if not the only sort deserving to be called thinking. One needs to know how one is to characterize the thinking of geographers, historians, creative artists, and so on. Is their thinking valid only to the degree that it is scientific? Surely this cannot be what Piaget intends? We must hope that Piaget will write the book for which Bruner asks in the review to which we referred earlier in this chapter, namely one that traces the development of the metaphorical thinking of play and dreams from childhood, through adolescence into adulthood.

Finally, let us see if we can summarize the reasons why Piaget's work has still had less impact on psychological thinking than its volume and originality would lead us to expect. The difficulties of mastering both Piaget's style and the logical model that he proposes have been mentioned, but it cannot be just these difficulties that have proved a stumbling block, for psychologists have come to grips with mathematical models in learning theory. Piaget's position is like that of Lewin (see Leeper, 1943). The terse comment by Peters (1966) that Piaget is expressing "logical truths dressed up in psychological guise, such as that learning must proceed from the simple to the complex, or that concrete operations with objects must precede abstract thought with them" is reminiscent of the objection commonly raised to Lewin's system, namely that it employs advanced mathematics to explain why an individual cannot go straight from *A* to *C* when *B* is in the way.

Piaget and Lewin have this in common that both attempt to construct an enclosed system in which all internal forces are accounted for rather than to elucidate the reaction of the system to outside forces. It is not in the nature of any science to treat of the whole universe of relevant concepts within one framework because every scientific system is bounded by reference to the concepts of other sciences. To the extent that Lewin and Piaget attempt to construct systems that attempt to explain all phenomena by reference to themselves, they are both essentially unscientific; however, the metaphysical characteristics of such systems are more marked in Piaget's case than that of Lewin.

There is within psychology a notable example of a self-contained system that has had a notable impact, namely psychoanalysis. Psychoanalytic concepts are not entirely self-contained, inasmuch as Freud thought of mental energy as deriving from physical energy, but given the source of the energy, the functioning of the psyche can be explained in terms of internal relationships. It is interesting to speculate on why Freud has had a greater impact than Lewin or Piaget. There appear to be two main reasons.

The first may be called "saving of conceptual effort". Psychology before Freud was concerned primarily with problems of consciousness such as sensation, perception, and cognition. Freud made psychology take account of emotions, and in particular of the unconscious component in human behaviour; in this way he was able to bring about a re-orientation of psychological thinking. Piaget is working within the field of cognition, and few psychologists see much advantage in re-orienting their thinking in an area in which concepts are already well established. Similarly, Lewin's concepts do not offer much promise of doing better the task that is already done by more orthodox notions.

The second point concerns the relationship between the explanatory system and what it is intended to explain. However esoteric Freud's concepts of id, ego, superego, libido, and so on may have seemed to psychologists at the turn of the century, it was clear, and it has remained clear, that Freud was concerned to explain the normal personality and deviations from it. Lewin and Piaget both occasionally give the impression that the models that they have constructed are more important in themselves than for what they explain. This objection can be raised with particular strength against Piaget, much of whose theoretical structure has the most tenuous connection with empirical findings. Whereas Freud implicitly asks "What can this system do for me?" Piaget seems to ask "What can I do with this system?"

What Piaget has done with his system, and why, it has been the object of this book to show. If this book has been successful, it will encourage students to go to the original works and discover more for themselves.

References

AUSUBEL, D. P. (1964) The transition from concrete to abstract cognitive functioning: theoretical issues and implications for education, *J. Res. Sci. Teaching* **2** (3), 261–6.

AYER, A. J. (1946) *Language, Truth, and Logic*, London, Victor Gollancz.

BALDWIN, A. L. (1967) *Theories of Child Development*, London, Wiley.

BETH, E. W. and PIAGET, J. (1966) *Mathematical Epistemology and Psychology*, Dordrecht, Reidel.

BORING, E. G. (1950) *A History of Experimental Psychology*, New York, Appleton–Century–Crofts.

BRIDGMAN, P. W. (1927) *The Logic of Modern Physics*, New York, MacMillan.

BRITTON, K. (1953) *John Stuart Mill*, Harmondsworth, Pelican Books, A274.

BROWN, J. A. C. (1961) *Freud and the Post-Freudians*, Harmondsworth, Pelican Books, A522.

BRUNER, J. S. (1959) Inhelder and Piaget's "The growth of logical thinking"; I, A psychologist's viewpoint, *Br. J. Psychol.* **50** (4), 363–70.

BRUNER, J. S. (1960) *The Process of Education*, Cambridge, Massachusetts, Harvard University Press.

BRUNER, J. S. (1964) The course of cognitive growth, *Am. Psychol.* **19** (1), 1–15. Reprinted in (ed.) Jones, R. M., *Contemporary Educational Psychology: Selected Readings*, New York, Harper & Row, pp. 123–55.

BRUNER, J. S., OLIVER, R. R., GREENFIELD, P. M. *et al.* (1966) *Studies in Cognitive Growth*, London, Wiley.

CONANT, J. B. (1956) *On Understanding Science: An Historical Approach*, New York, New American Library (Mentor Books).

CRONBACH, L. J. (1964) Learning research and curriculum development, *J. Res. Sci. Teaching* **2** (3), 204–7.

DIENES, Z. P. (1960) *Building Up Mathematics*, London, Hutchinson Educational Press.

DOLLARD, J. and MILLER, N. E. (1950) *Personality and Psychotherapy: An Analysis in Terms of Learning, Thinking, and Culture*, London, McGraw-Hill.

FLAVELL, J. H. (1963) *The Developmental Psychology of Jean Piaget*, Princeton, New Jersey, D. Van Nostrand (University Series in Psychology), with a foreword by J. Piaget.

FURTH, H. G. (1966) *Thinking Without Language: Psychological Implications of Deafness*, London, Collier–MacMillan.

GHISELIN, B. (Ed.) (1952) *The Creative Process: A Symposium*, New York, New American Library (Mentor Books).

HALL, C. S. and LINDZEY, G. (1957) *Theories of Personality*, London, Wiley.

INHELDER, B., BOVET, M., and SMOCK, C. D. (1966) On cognitive development, *Am. Psychol.* **21** (2), 160–4.

INHELDER, B., and PIAGET, J. (1958) *The Growth of Logical Thinking from Childhood to Adolescence: An Essay on the Construction of Formal Operational Structures*, London, Routledge and Kegan Paul.

ISAACS, N. (1960) *New Light on Children's Ideas of Number: The Work of Professor Piaget*, London, Ward Lock Educational Company.

ISAACS, N. (1961) *The Growth of Understanding in the Young Child: A Brief Introduction to Piaget's Work*, London, Ward Lock Educational Company.

ISAACS, N. (1966) The wider significance of Piaget's work *and* Piaget and progressive education, in *Some Aspects of Piaget's Work*, London, National Froebel Foundation.

KILPATRICK, J. (1964) Cognitive theory and the school mathematics study group program, *J. Res. Sci. Teaching* **2** (3), 247–51.

KLINE, M. (1953) *Mathematics in Western Culture*, New York, Oxford University Press.

LEEPER, R. W. (1943) *Lewin's Topological and Vector Psychology*, Eugene, Oregon, University of Oregon Press.

LOVELL, K. (1961) *The Growth of Mathematical and Scientific Concepts in Children*, London, University of London Press.

LUNZER, E. A. (1962) *Recent Studies in Britain Based on the Work of Jean Piaget*, London, National Foundation for Educational Research in England and Wales.

LURIA, A. R. (1961) *The Role of Speech in the Regulation of Normal and Abnormal Behaviour*, New York, Pergamon Press.

MAIER, H. W. (1965) *Three Theories of Child Development: The Contributions of Erik H. Erikson, Jean Piaget and Robert R. Sears, and Their Applications*, New York, Harper & Row (Harper International Student Reprints).

MAYS, W. (1954) The epistemology of Professor Piaget, *Proc. Aristotelian Soc.* **54**, 49–76.

MINK, O. G. (1964) Experience and cognitive structure, *J. Res. Sci. Teaching* **2** (3), 196–203.

PARSONS, C. (1960) Inhelder and Piaget's "The growth of logical thinking"; II, A logician's viewpoint, *Br. J. Psychol.* **51** (1), 75–84.

PEEL, E. A. (1960) *The Pupil's Thinking*, London, Oldbourne.

PETERS, R. S. (1966) *Ethics and Education*, London, Allen & Unwin.

PIAGET, J. (1950a) *Introduction à l'épistémologie génétique*, Paris, Presses Universitaires de France.

PIAGET, J. (1950b) *The Psychology of Intelligence*, London, Routledge and Kegan Paul.

PIAGET, J. (1953a) *Logic and Psychology*, Manchester, Manchester University Press.

PIAGET, J. (1953b) *The Origin of Intelligence in the Child*, London, Routledge and Kegan Paul.

PIAGET, J. (1959) *The Language and Thought of the Child*, London, Routledge and Kegan Paul.

PIAGET, J. (1962) *Comments on Vygotsky's Critical Remarks Concerning "The Language and Thought of the Child" and "Judgement and Reasoning in the Child"*, Cambridge, Massuchusetts, Massachusetts Institute of Technology Press.

PIAGET, J. (1964) Development and learning, *J. Res. Sci. Teaching.* **2** (3), 176–86.

PIAGET, J. and INHELDER, B. (1968) *Mémoire et intelligence*, Paris, Presses Universitaires de France.

PINARD, A. and LAURENDEAU, M. (1964) A scale of mental development based on the theory of Jean Piaget: description of a project, *J. Res. Sci. Teaching* **2** (3), 253–60.

RIPPLE, R. E. (1964) American cognitive studies: a review, *J. Res. Sci. Teaching* **2** (3), 187–95.

SAPORTA, S. (Ed.) (1961) *Psycholinguistics: A Book of Readings*, New York, Holt, Rinehart & Winston.

SMEDSLUND, J. (1964) Internal necessity and contradiction in children's thinking, *J. Res. Sci. Teaching* **2** (3), 220–1.

TOULMIN, S. (1961) *Foresight and Understanding: An Enquiry into the Aims of Science*, London, Hutchinson, with a foreword by J. Barzun.

VERNON, P. E. (1960) *Intelligence and Attainment Tests*, London, University of London Press.

VERNON, P. E. (1964) *Personality Assessment: A Critical Survey*, London, Methuen.

VYGOTSKY, L. S. (1962) *Thought and Language*, Cambridge, Massachusetts, Massachusetts Institute of Technology Press.

WOODWARD, M. (1959) The behaviour of idiots interpreted by Piaget's theory of sensorimotor development, *Br. J. Educ. Psychol.* **29,** 60–71.

Suggestions for Further Reading

BREARLEY, M. and HITCHFIELD, E. (1966) *A Teacher's Guide to Reading Piaget*, London, Routledge and Kegan Paul (Routledge Paperbacks). Contains selections from Piaget's work on number, measurement, knots, perspective, co-ordinates, floating and sinking, moral judgement, and the behaviour of babies.

FLEW, A. (1962) *David Hume on Human Nature and the Understanding: Edited with an Introduction and an Annotated Index*, London, Collier–MacMillan.

GRENE, M. (1963) *A Portrait of Aristotle*, London, Faber & Faber.

INHELDER, B. and PIAGET, J. (1964) *The Early Growth of Logic in the Child*, London, Routledge and Kegan Paul.

KÖRNER, S. (1955) *Kant*, Harmondsworth, Pelican Books, A338.

LUCAS, P. G. (1953) *Immanuel Kant: Prolegomena to any Future Metaphysics that will be able to Represent itself as a Science: A Translation with Introduction and Notes*, Manchester, Manchester University Press.

O'CONNOR, D. J. (1952) *John Locke*, Harmondsworth, Pelican Books, A267.

PIAGET, J. (1953c). How children form mathematical concepts. *Scientific American*, reprinted in Mussen, P. H., Conger, J. J., and Kagan, J. *Readings in Child Development and Personality*, New York, Harper & Row, pp. 304–312.

TOULMIN, S. (1953) *The Philosophy of Science*, London, Hutchinson (Grey Arrow Editions, 1962).

WARNOCK, G. J. (1953) *Berkeley*, Harmondsworth, Pelican Books, A286.

Name Index

151

Subject Index

153